# Radiant

# Radiant

## Discovering Beauty
## from the Inside Out

Chandra Peele

NEW HOPE
PUBLISHERS

Birmingham, Alabama

New Hope® Publishers
P. O. Box 12065
Birmingham, AL 35202-2065
www.newhopepublishers.com

Library of Congress Cataloging-in-Publication Data

Peele, Chandra.
  Radiant : discovering beauty from the inside out / Chandra Peele.
    p. cm.
  ISBN 978-1-59669-089-9 (sc)
  1. Spirituality—Textbooks. 2. Christian life—Textbooks. I. Title.
BV4501.3.P437 2007
248.4—dc22

                    2006039258

ISBN-13: 978-1-59669-089-9
ISBN-10: 1-59669-089-5

N076126 • 0607 • 4M1

# Dedication

This study is affectionately dedicated to my daughters,
Lindsey and Holly

My joy is complete in Christ
And then . . . there's the two of you;
two cherries on top of my very sweet and blessed life.

And I also dedicate this book to Bruce, my loving husband.
I wouldn't have our precious daughters if I didn't have you.
What a wonderful life!

For joy is life in excess,
the overflow of what cannot be
contained within any one person!
(The Message) Introduction Philippians

*I love you so much! I do want the very best for you.*
*You make me feel such joy, fill me with such pride.*
*Don't waver. Stay on track, steady in God.*
—Philippians 4:1 (The Message)

# Table of Contents

Introduction ................................................................9

Session One: **Real World—Real God** ............................15

Session Two: **The Transformation** .............................45

Session Three: **The Real YOU!** .................................67

Session Four: **Heir to the King** ................................79

Session Five: **The Beauty and the Beast in Me** ...........97

Session Six: **The Condition of Your Heart** ................ 119

A Few Last Words ................................................... 149

More GAB Sessions. .................................................. 155

# introduction

My first passion in life is being a wife and a mom. My second is encouraging others to live the exciting and abundant life found in Jesus. And third, I really enjoy redecorating homes for people who are ready for a change.

I am asked to come in and redecorate often because clients have become bored with their home. The first thing I do is set up a consultation so we can discuss what they like and don't like about their home or a particular room. Next, I ask them what they like most about their home. Then we discuss style. From traditional to contemporary, some clients know their style while others simply have no style—they like everything.

An interview with the client gives me a taste of who they are, as well as their likes and dislikes. Then I ask the most important question of all, "What do you want your home to reflect to your family and guests when they step inside?"

Most Christian women want their home to feel warm and inviting, like the feeling you get when you smell chocolate chip cookies baking in the oven on a chilly day while the fireplace is crackling and popping from the dry wood burning.

Comfort is the second most common request. Like beauty, comfort can be different for each person. Once a client defines comfort, my goal is to make it happen. My job as her designer is to recognize what she needs and make it hers.

Next, we set a date and time to get rid of the items no longer needed. After we've taken out all the old, we are ready to fill it with the new. Then I begin to create a warm, inviting, comfortable, and happy space.

Now, I go shopping. This is really fun! But it also requires a lot of thinking and a lot of work. After the new items are selected, I'm ready to do the install. Some people like to call it the "makeover." The client trusts me completely and is never at home when I do this. This gives me the freedom to use my gifts to complete the task. Once everything is in its place, I call my client and say, "Come on home."

The most rewarding moment for me is when she opens the door and her face looks like she's just walked into a surprise party. Speechless, she walks around the room taking in everything. From new accent pillows, new rugs, lamps, the new painting on the wall to the smallest accessory; she doesn't want to miss a single detail. She is satisfied! She loves it! My job is complete.

What about your house? No, not the houses you live in but the house that is inside you. (*"Do you not know that your body is a temple of the Holy Spirit, who is in you, whom you have received from God? You are not your own; you were bought at a price. Therefore, honor God with your body"* —1 Corinthians 6: 19–20).

Are there items in your inner house that are old and need to be cleaned out? Perhaps your taste has changed, and you realize you are still storing all that old junk. Maybe it's time for a consultation with the best Designer of all, God, our Creator. (*"Therefore, if anyone is in Christ, He is a new creation; the old has gone, the new has come!"* —2 Corinthians 5:17).

With Christ living in us, even on days when it's pouring down rain outside, it's a bright sunny day in our hearts. (For God, who said, (*"'Let light shine out of darkness,' made his light shine in our hearts to give us the light of the knowledge of the glory of God in the face of Christ"* —2 Corinthians 4:6.)

This book is about change. As a young woman who already knows Jesus Christ, hopefully you'll be challenged, sharpened, and refined as you read through the pages. Or, if you are searching for that something or someone to satisfy you, to brighten your life, to give you a sense of purpose, you'll find that here too.

God our Father calls the church, the bride of Christ. As we live each day seeking His wisdom and having a heart that desires to glorify Him, we become more and more like Him. We are preparing to meet the bridegroom, Jesus. The closer we get to Him, the more we communicate with Him, the more we read about Him, and the more we reflect Him. That is when we become the radiant bride.

When you think of radiant, what are your thoughts? One who stands out? One who seems bright and joyful? Have you been to a wedding and heard someone say: "The bride is beautiful! She's glowing! She is radiant!"?

As I watch the bride walk down the aisle, my eyes usually fill with tears. There's just something unexplainable about the beauty of the bride. How wonderful that God would call us "the bride."

Throughout the book, you will have the opportunity to reflect on certain situations, to pray, read your Bibles, and write responses to certain questions. You can move through the book at our own speed. You can use the

*Synonyms: beaming, beamy, radiating or as if radiating light, glowing, bright, energy, luminous, shiny, lustrous.*

*It's important to recognize the opposite of radiant.*

*Antonyms are: Cloudy, dark, dim, dull, gloomy, sad.*

journal section to write thoughts or perhaps you would like to write in your personal journal.

Here's an exercise to do before beginning Session One. Are you ready to become radiant for Him?
Let's imagine the Master Designer, God, has asked you: What would you like your inner house to reflect?

Contemplate your answer, and then write your response below or in a journal.

❖

*Let's imagine the Master Designer, God, has asked you: What would you like your inner house to reflect?*

_____

_____

_____

_____

_____

_____

_____

_____

_____

_____

_____

_____

_____

Now, are you ready to get the job done? Trust your Master Designer, God, to make whatever changes are necessary to prepare you for a bright future as you complete your purpose. Get ready to see a whole new you as the power of the Holy Spirit works His makeover in you.

Oh, yes, I have an hourly fee for my design time. God, however, is always available for us to call on any time of the day or night. His love, wisdom, and direction are free. I guess we could say it comes with His package. (*"Now to him who is able to do immeasurably more than all we ask or imagine, according to his power at work within us, to him be glory in the church and in Christ Jesus throughout all generations, for ever and ever! Amen"* —Ephesians 3:20–21.)

# Real World–Real God

Yes, we live in it. No question that the good, the bad, and the ugly are all around us. However, we can't go through life wearing blinders. It just doesn't work that way. And if we did, what freedom would be found in that? But we can realize that most of what we see and hear is not what God intended. When God created the world, imagine how pure and perfect it was. Well, that didn't last long. Adam and Eve fell into Satan's trap and the rest is history. Now our grandparents, parents, brothers, and sisters, and all those who come after us must live in this sinful world.

The good news is that God sent us a Savior, His one and only Son, Jesus Christ. We can choose to follow His path instead of the world's way. Yes, the temptation is great with everything from raunchy movies, to vulgar music, and porn at the tips of our fingers. So let's face it. It's easy to be bad, and oh so hard to be good. That is why we need His help every moment of our lives. If we believe that Jesus Christ is the Son of God, then we are believers. We are Christ followers, Christians. If Christ is in us, then we have His strength and power to make God-honoring choices.

*Holy Spirit: When Jesus left this earth to be with God the Father in heaven, He sent the Holy Spirit to dwell in those who would accept Him as the Messiah, the Son of the one and only true God. Those who by faith believe are empowered with the Holy Spirit as a counselor and guide.*
(*Priceless* by Chandra Peele, p. 16)

## Keep Watch!

God knew we would struggle with temptation, and in Matthew, chapter 4, we can see that even Jesus experienced temptation. Open your Bible now, and read Matthew 4. Jesus had gone to the desert to be alone, and He was there for 40 days and 40 nights. Jesus became hungry and weak. He was distracted! Satan was waiting.

Satan attacks us when we are weak and off guard. Satan is always ready. He knows where and when we're weak and can cause doubt and confusion when we're making choices. Satan is a coward. He's evil and just waits for us to mess up. Just as Jesus told Satan to get away from Him, we too can rebuke Satan.

> *Away from me, Satan!" For it is written: 'Worship the Lord your God, and serve him only.' Then the devil left him, and angels came and attended him.* —Matthew 4:10.

Satan is sneaky and often uses others to convince us to try things we know are not honoring God. We may think we would never fall into his trap, but let's take a really good look at the world around us.

We are bombarded with temptation every day. If we're not spiritually prepared, the temptation may be too great for us to resist. Then in our human weaknesses, we rationalize the situation until it seems OK. We have become pretty good at twisting the Scripture and watering it down to make it fit our selfish desires. Our flesh is weak, and in the blink of an eye we may find ourselves stepping into the "Sin Zone." Next we ask, "What was I thinking?" Or, maybe, "What am I doing?"

*"Away from me, Satan!"*

How we disappoint ourselves by making a decision to join in the crowd just because everyone else did! For example, we go to a party that involves drugs and alcohol, we start to smoke, steal items from stores, use bad language, gossip, tell a dirty joke, disobey our parents, or wear an inappropriate outfit to get attention.

Temptations will come and go, but how do you handle them when they come? Make a list of things that often tempt you.

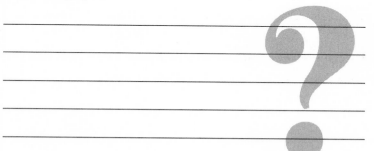

## Temptation: The Mall

Answer the following questions and think about how you can avoid these temptations. Write your responses.

**Are you tempted to overspend when you go to the mall? How can you avoid this behavior?**

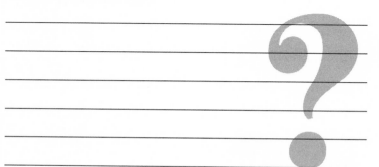

*How we disappoint ourselves by making a decision to join in the crowd just because everyone else did!*

Have you bought something knowing you really didn't have the money? How can you avoid this behavior?

_____

_____

_____

_____

_____

Have you ever stolen merchandise from a store? How can you avoid this behavior?

_____

_____

_____

_____

In what other areas do you need to practice self-control when you are at the mall?

_____

_____

_____

_____

_____

# Temptation: Celebrity Craze

In today's society, many young people are starstruck. We are a media-based society and always seem to be plugged into something. Morning, noon, or primetime viewers have a plethora of shows sharing every move popular celebrities make. Viewers can see anything from what celebrities are wearing; whom they are dating; and where they are living, shopping, and eating.

Unfortunately, many young people today are influenced by these celebrities and are tempted to act like them too. But many of those celebrities that young people emulate are not good Christian role models. Who and what do these celebrities reflect? What kind of influence do they have on us?

The reality is that Hollywood is a fantasy world. As children of God we need to recognize we can easily be tempted because Satan is the deceiver, and he enjoys watching God's people get hooked, especially onto something that looks so good, but isn't. It's the thrill of Hollywood that is so enticing. Everyone and everything about it looks so fun and exciting! Then in the midst of our fantasy life we slowly begin to think our home, our clothes, our parents, our friends just aren't good enough for us. These thoughts can lead us to an ugly and ungodly attitude that screams: *I'm better than everyone else. I deserve the best. I. I. I. I. I.* We can become more and more selfish and unrealistic as we journey into self-centeredness.

So, how can we watch and read about celebrities and not be tempted? We need to be strong in the Lord. This will help our mind filter what we read and see. So, how can we be strong in the Lord?

*I'm better than everyone else. I deserve the best.*

**Open your Bible and read Ephesians 6:10-18.**

Write down what God's full armor is and how it fits you.

_____

_____

_____

_____

_____

## A Positive Influence or A Negative Influence?

Thankfully there are some Christian brothers and sisters on the movie screen who do not live the Hollywood glitz. They want to live their lives, raise their families, and be "normal." They are known by their peers to have godly character and integrity. We are also blessed with talented and creative Christian artists whose music moves us closer to God. But remember they are people and God loves them, just as He loves us. They make mistakes, just like we do. They need a Savior, just like we do.

Today many of us live in a fantasy world and constantly compare ourselves to famous celebrities. We want to look like celebrities, dress like them, live like them, and often go to the extreme to be them. We think they are perfect and we are not. We should not have a sense of failure when we don't have what the world says are the perfect teeth, the perfect wardrobe, the perfect hair, or the perfect weight. Life is so much more than being caught-up in this material world. And remember, there

*What you put in*

*is what comes out!*

is no one on this earth who is perfect. Jesus Christ was the only man ever to walk on the earth who was perfect. So quit trying to keep up. Enjoy life. Commit that you will learn to like "the me" that God created.

Answer the following questions and write down your responses.

**Are you consumed with a particular celebrity? Why?**

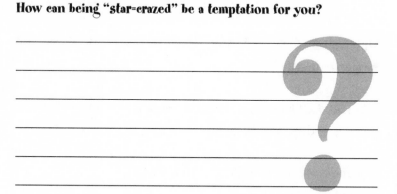

_____

_____

_____

_____

_____

**How can being "star-crazed" be a temptation for you?**

_____

_____

_____

_____

_____

**How can watching the lifestyles of the rich and famous impact your life?**

_____

_____

_____

_____

_____

**What do you like about yourself? Dislike? How can you overcome the dislikes?**

_____

_____

_____

_____

_____

**Open your Bible and read these verses. Mark them, and memorize them.**

> *You shall have no other gods before me.*
> —Exodus 20:3

> *You shall not make for yourself an idol."*
> —Exodus 20:4

Now let's reflect on God's Word. Read Psalm 139, and then spend time reflecting on who God made you to be. Praise God that you are wonderfully made.

# Temptation: Makeover Mania!

There's no question our culture enjoys a good makeover program. The American dream is no longer only about owning your own home and driving a car that's paid for, but now we've become obsessed with improving our bodies with injections of Botox, surgery, and finding the ultimate diet pill to experience perfection. We love to see the "before" and ooh and aah when the "after" is revealed. What these television programs fail to disclose is that this is only a makeover for the outside; a temporary fix of sorts. Although there has been a dramatic change on the outside, true beauty can only be found from the inside out. After hours of primping from a makeup artist, hairstylist, and wardrobe stylist, any of us could look red-carpet flawless. But, is this going to make us happy? Maybe temporarily, but what most of us really want is that deep-down-inside kind of happiness.

Think about your uniqueness and real beauty—the kind from within. You will never find true happiness if your external life is beautiful but your inner life is a mess. The best beauty tip is—be you!

Take a minute to answer these questions. Be honest!

**How is your relationship with Jesus?**

**Are you reading His Word?**

**Are you talking with Him? Are you listening to Him?**

**Are you giving away some of your time, money, and gifts?**

Take a closer look at your life. Who or what are you reflecting at school, at home, at your job, at your church, on your emails?

*You will never find true happiness if your external life is beautiful but your inner life is a mess.*

When we choose to reflect worldliness instead of god-liness, our hearts will become inflated like a balloon that becomes so puffed up there is nothing it can do except POP! When we hit the ground, it's going to hurt! Why wait for that to happen? We can begin to deflate our puffed-up heart today by admitting our self-centeredness.

**When people look at you, what do they see? Write your answer below.**

_____

_____

_____

_____

*Do not store up treasures on earth, where moths and rust destroy, and where thieves break in and steal. But store up for yourselves treasures in heaven, where moth and rust do not destroy, and where thieves do not break in and steal. For where your treasure is, there your heart will be also.*
—Matthew 6:19–21

**Open your Bible and read Matthew 6:19-34. What does it say to you?**

_____

_____

_____

_____

_____

## Temptation: Our Eyes, Ears, and Minds

What if we look at suggestive pictures, read certain articles in magazines, or watch adult-oriented prime-time TV? We may have mixed feelings about right and wrong. We begin to rationalize that everything is immoral. Then we talk about what we have read, seen, or heard with our friends, and it becomes easier and easier to make immorality sound OK. The jokes and laughter make it all seem like no big deal. This may be just the beginning, but if we continue to ignore the Holy Spirit that lives within us, we'll soon become calloused to the harm of what we are putting in our minds. We may say things like, "Everyone's doing it, " or "It's the style now," or "Oh well, that's life in the new millennium." "No harm done, right?"

Well, let's think about that.

## Stand Firm!

We read in 1 Peter 5:8–9: *"Be self-controlled and alert. Your enemy the devil prowls like a roaring lion looking for someone to devour. Resist him, standing firm in the faith, because you know that your brothers throughout the world are undergoing the same kind of sufferings."*

Jesus gives a great example of guarding our thoughts. In our weakness we can become vulnerable to Satan's attacks. We should keep our eyes on Christ, not the materialistic "stuff" and idealistic lifestyle of the world.

Sometimes I have the opportunity to meet with small groups of girls. A couple of the activities that I share with them involves pictures I have cut from magazines. We can do this activity too. Let's see if there are some areas where we have become calloused.

**For activity one, you'll need magazines and scissors.
For activity two, you will need scissors, glue, magazines, a
piece of paper or a shoebox, and a few markers.**

**Activity One:** Look through some magazines for articles and advertisements that use sex or sensuality to get your attention. As you cut them out, you will begin to recognize how much you have become immune to immorality, which is so commonly portrayed in the media today. Since you do read magazines, go to movies, watch television, and, of course, listen to music, this project is designed to raise your awareness. You may find it hard to notice these articles and advertisements when you begin, but as you flip through the pages, watch and listen with your spiritual eyes.

**Activity Two:** Cut out pictures in the magazine that portray you. If you have a camera available, take some fun pictures of yourself just being YOU. Now add things that describe you such as your favorite color, pet, food, sports, and so forth. Next glue all your pictures to a box or paper and keep it somewhere safe where you can pull it out and look at it every once in a while. That way, you'll have something to remind you of who you are. On the top of the paper or the lid of your box write in big letters *VIP, Very Important Princess*. You can put this box in your room to keep special notes in or perhaps notes you write to God. If you make a poster, hang it on your wall. Whichever you choose, each time you look at it be reminded that you are a very important Princess and that God, the Creator of the universe, not only made you, but He loves you just the way you are.

We live in a very real world. Since we can't take ourselves out of it, we need to be confident that we more importantly serve a very real God. (*"Above all else, guard your heart, for it is the wellspring of life"* —Proverbs 4:23)

As Christians, we are the light God uses to radiate His love to a world filled with darkness (sin).

**Open your Bible and read Matthew 5:14-16, and then answer these questions.**
In what ways are you recognizably "the light of the world"?
What are some specific ways you can shine brighter to reflect Christ? At home? At school? In your neighborhood?
Are you aware of times when Christians turn their backs or hide in the seclusion of their homes? How does this relate to the teaching in verse 15.

**Open your Bible and read John 1:1-5.**
*In the beginning was the Word, and the Word was with God, and the Word was God. He was with God in the beginning. Through him all things were made; without him nothing was made that has been made. In him was life, and that life was the light of men. The light shines in the darkness, but the darkness has not understood it.*

Verse 10 tells us, "He was in the world, and though the world was made through him, the world did not recognize him." Verse 14 says, "The Word became flesh and made his dwelling among us. We have seen his glory, the glory of the One and Only, who came from the Father, full of grace and truth."

He was radiant.

## How Can We Become Radiant?

Jesus is our example. We should desire to reflect Him to the world. It's obvious that hiding our light, hiding behind our Christian values, is not what Jesus did. God is love. Jesus, His Son, reflects that love. When we draw close to the Son, we become radiant as we reflect Him to the world.

Each of us will experience times of heartache and pain in this life, Christian or not. These "not so pretty" experiences or "dark times in life" are often just the thing God can use to make us shine brighter and reflect Him more.

*We could never be brave and patient, if there were only joy in the world.*
*—Helen Keller*

In every experience good or bad, we will choose how it affects our lives. You've probably heard this age-old saying, "It can make you bitter or better."

There is a lot of truth in those seven words. When you experienced difficult times, what choices did you make? How did you handle those times?

**Think about the following and write about each of these times. What made the difference?**

*"We could never be brave and patient, if there were only joy in the world."*
*Helen Keller*

A time that made me bitter:

_____

_____

_____

_____

A time that made me better:

_____

_____

_____

_____

Philippians 2:14–16 puts it so clearly. *"Do everything without complaining or arguing, so that you may become blameless and pure, children of God without fault in a crooked and depraved generation, in which you shine like stars in the universe as you hold out the word of life—in order that I may boast on the day of Christ and that I did not run or labor for nothing."*

Does your life "shine like stars"? Have you ever been outside on a beautiful sunny, blue-sky day when all at once a huge white puffy cloud shielded the sun and blocked the light? Maybe you have allowed a moment, an ugly word, gossip, or jealousy to be the cloud in your life that has blocked the Son from shining through. If you're standing under a cloud, move! Find the Son.

*Does your life*

*"shine like stars"?*

When He shines on you, you'll become radiant to all those around. You'll be transformed into the likeness of Christ Jesus, the One who shines through you.

## A Life-Changing Choice

There is a story in the Bible about a woman who fell into the schemes of darkness. By the world's standards she became an outcast in her day. Take a moment to read her story in John 4:1–42. We see how after being in the presence of the Son, she made a choice and was changed.

- She was a Samaritan woman.
- The Samaritan people were a hated mixed race.
- Quickly we find that she had a bad reputation in her town because she lived a life of infidelity.
- We see that Jesus was openly talking to her. He asked her for a drink. It's important to note that this was not a common thing. In fact, Jewish people were never seen with the Samaritan people.

Careful not to pass by the other women, the Samaritan woman went to fill her jars in the hottest part of the day. Knowing the whispering, dirty looks, and gossip would only hurt again, she stayed out of sight as much as possible. When she arrived at the well, Jesus was there and asked her for a drink. Little did she know, this would be the day her life would change! On this day she met the Messiah. She chose to believe. She drank from the Living Well, Jesus! He knew everything about her, yet He still offered His forgiveness and grace to her. His love for her and the grace He showed her was greater than her ugly past. She was changed! She ran back to her town a new person. She laid her burdens down. She left her sin with Jesus. He took the weight off her shoulders. She was restored! Joyful! Because of her excitement and zeal, others were curious. In verse 39 of this chapter, the Bible tells us, *"Many of the Samaritans from that town believed in him because of the woman's testimony, 'He told me everything I ever did.'"*

Unfortunately, some of our stories may be similar to the Samaritan woman's. The culture is different. Perhaps our sin is different. But the hurt we have felt is the same. The shame we carry from past sin has made us feel like an outcast. Jesus is still setting people free from the bondage sin brings. The Samaritan woman made a choice. She made a choice to believe in the Messiah. We can make the same choice today. Will we continue to live defeated? Or, will we choose to live in the freedom experienced on earth only through Jesus? The choice is ours to make.

**Do you have a story to share? Has Jesus changed your life? Write it down and look for opportunities to share it later.**

My story is about _____

_____

_____

_____

_____

_____

_____

*Grace—Grace is a gift. The greatest gift of all is eternal life through Jesus. He died on the cross so that you might live forever!*
(*Priceless* by Chandra Peele, p. 15)

_____

_____

_____

_____

_____

_____

_____

_____

_____

## Reality!

I have found that girls who experience a terrible, hurtful, and sometimes abusive home life often end up choosing the same kind of relationships when they get older. It's strange, however very common. This helps protect their hearts. If they never face the facts, never admit how bad things were in their childhoods, then they never have to deal with the pain. Instead they push the hurt down and allow their past to direct their future. These girls may have never known a loving relationship from parents. They may have never seen their parents pray for each other, tenderly love on each other, and show kindness to one another and to the family. Instead they are used to screaming and banging and demanding. Sometimes they have been exposed to drugs.

Some of us may relate to this kind of lifestyle. Or, maybe we can see the path we are on is headed for this kind of life. If so, write your responses to the following statements. These are things in my life that I do not like:

_____

_____

_____

_____

_____

_____

I no longer want to live this way, but I want to be like:

_____

_____

_____

_____

_____

_____

I admit I need God in my life because:

_____

_____

_____

_____

_____

_____

I need God to give me direction in my life for:

_____

_____

_____

_____

_____

_____

Spend time in quiet reflection of your past. Imagine letting it go and giving it to God. Wow! Guess what? God has it now. You are a new person in Jesus. Live your life accordingly.

In this dark and real world we live in, choose the very real and only God. In Him there is hope! With Him your life will change directions.

Jesus said, *"Anyone who is thirsty may come to me! Anyone who believes in me may come and drink! For the Scriptures declare, 'rivers of living water will flow from his heart'"* (John 7:37–38 NLT).

Jesus says, *"If you only knew the gift God has for you and who I am, you would ask me, and I would give you living water"* (John 4:10 NLT).

**Let's review.** The Samaritan woman was stuck in the miry yuck and muck of this world; her joy was gone from the guilt of her past. I'm sure in her loneliness she wondered if her life would ever get better. Could it be this was the life she deserved? Absolutely NOT!

What a perfect time to read John 10:10 again! *"The thief's purpose is to steal and kill and destroy. My purpose is to give them a rich and satisfying life"* (NLT).

Satan wants us to have bad thoughts. He wants to crush our spirits and make our lives miserable. But Jesus Christ comes to seek and save the lost! He comes so that we would have life to the fullest! Isn't that exciting?

There is no question the Samaritan woman's life changed after meeting Jesus. When she ran to tell the people in her community about Jesus, she didn't stop and ask, "What will they think of me?"

No! Meeting Jesus and believing He was the Messiah changed her from the inside out. She was radiant the day she shared the good news; it was overflowing. Jesus had given her hope, and she was experiencing joy for the first time in a long, long time. She couldn't contain herself. She had to tell them. The people knew who she was, but it was evident she was a changed woman.

**Would you like to experience change like this in your life?**
Stop and pray. Ask the Lord to bless you with a full life. Tell Him your hurts. Then give them over to Him. You may want to write down what you feel. Or, perhaps find a place where you can talk to God out loud. Have a conversation with Him. Empty your hurts. He is listening.

Ask Jesus to come into your heart, to change your life, and to help you become more like Him. Then follow through by reading and studying God's Word. Find a place where you enjoy going to learn more about Jesus. Join your local church, attend a Bible study, or join a prayer group. Radiate His love.

*When Satan comes back over and taps you on the shoulder to remind you of the past, say the name of Jesus out loud. Tell Satan to flee from you, just like Jesus did in the garden. Watch how quickly Satan leaves.*

*Dear Lord,*

*thank You for Your*

*unconditional love.*

*Thank You for Your*

*gift of grace through*

*Jesus. I pray that today*

*You will fill me with*

*Your love.*

*Lord, teach me through*

*Your Word so I will*

*reflect You in my*

*actions and my speech.*

*Lord, when I am*

*tempted, help me make*

*godly choices.*

**FYI**—When Satan comes back over and taps you on the shoulder to remind you of the past, say the name of Jesus out loud. Tell Satan to flee from you, just like Jesus did in the garden. Watch how quickly Satan leaves.

As Christians, we need to believe in the hope we have in Jesus. When we experience freedom and joy for ourselves, then we can share our story with others. Many times a story, perhaps your story, is just the thing God can use. How will others know if we don't tell them? Think about it. What has Jesus done for you? Do you have a story to share?

**Write it out, and then share it with someone.**

_____

_____

_____

_____

_____

_____

_____

_____

_____

_____

_____

_____

_____

*When I am weak and*
*confused by the schemes*
*of worldly darkness,*
*I know in Your*
*presence I am strong.*
*I pray in the name of*
*Jesus for Satan to get*
*away from me. I pray*
*that I will run from evil*
*and impurity and all*
*unholy thoughts. I seek*
*the power of Your Holy*
*Spirit to keep me in*
*Your will.*
*Amen.*

# GAB Session
## ~ with Chandra ~

**M**atthew, Mark, Luke, and John are called the Gospel books of the Bible. They present the life of Christ to us. We learn about the character of Jesus as we read these books. As we read and study these books of the Bible, we learn how Jesus showed His love to others.

We discover that Jesus hung out with, ate with, and spoke with people that were not in the popular crowd. In fact, some of the people He hung out with were "bad people" in the eyes of others.

So here is the point. We are all like those so-called bad people without the grace and forgiveness of Jesus Christ. Only through Jesus can we love others unconditionally. Only through Jesus can we understand forgiveness. Only through Jesus can we be content and happy in the real world.

# My Journal

We've looked at a lot in this session.
- Worldly temptation
- Satan's deception
- Celebrities and how they impact your life
- The importance of guarding your life with the full armor of God
- The ugly reality
- The choice to change

Now, let's write about the negative effects the world has on us and what choices we can make to guard our lives from these worldly ways. Include thoughts about ignoring and becoming calloused to the immorality we see all around us. Write your responses below or in a personal journal.

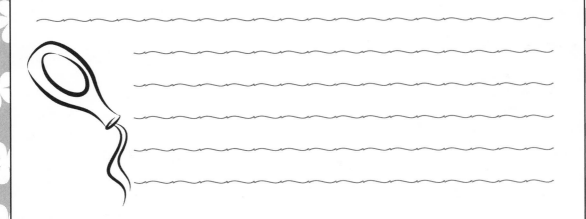

# My Journal

# My Journal

# My Journal

# My Journal

# My Journal

## session 2

# The Transformation

Billy Graham tells this story.

There was a woman and she loved her pig. She went out to the pigpen and brought the pig into her house. She bathed the pig and put perfume on the pig. She dressed the pig in a froufrou little outfit and then tied a bow around its head.

When her husband came home for dinner, the pig was sitting at the table. The man said, "What is that pig doing at my table?"

The wife replied that the pig had been changed. "Honey, I have given the pig a bath and put clothes on it. I have taught it to sit at the table and have trained it to behave in the house. We have a new pig," she exclaimed.

The man got up from the table, went to the door, and told the pig to get out of the house. Much to the surprise of the wife, the pig ran straight back to the pigpen and rolled around in the mud squealing all the way home. With this, the man said to the wife, "Once a pig, always a pig."

**Open your Bible and read 2 Corinthians 3:18.**

*And we, who with unveiled faces all reflect the Lord's glory, are being transformed into his likeness with ever-increasing glory, which comes from the Lord, who is the Spirit.*

You see, being born again happens from the inside out. The change is in your heart. Unfortunately there are many people who only pretend to be Christian.

## Read: Matthew 7:21-27.

The change comes from within. No one gets extra points with God for doing a lot of "stuff." It doesn't make Him love us any more or any less. God looks at the purity of the heart.

The world would agree with the idea of dressing up the pig. If it looks good and acts good, it must be good. Nope! Thank goodness God doesn't look at the brand of jeans we wear or the neighborhood where we live. He looks at our hearts.

Are we like the pig? Playing Christianity and pretending to be Christians? Hoping we're good enough to earn a ticket to heaven? Or, are we living it out loud?

## Madison's Story

Sitting in the airport awaiting my flight I filled my boredom with "people watching." It wasn't long before I did a double take. A young woman covered in body art stopped at my gate. Tattoos on her calves, arms, and neck! A funky little haircut . . . umm . . . actually it was kind of cute. *How sad*, I thought to myself. *Why did she do that to herself? What a beautiful girl she could be.*

She began talking to a girl who had been standing across from me for quite some time. Of course I had noticed her cute trendy outfit and adorable haircut already. After watching them for a few moments, I realized I was staring and quickly turned in the other direction. My daughters call it the two-minute rule. Looking at one thing more than two minutes is called staring, and it's not polite. They are absolutely correct.

Pretending to read the newspaper, my ears were intently eavesdropping on their conversation. What? I heard the word *Jesus*. You know there is no other name like it, so I knew; I just knew that sweet young trendy girl had to be witnessing to the tattoo girl. Soon they called my flight for boarding. I quickly gathered my bags, threw away the spoon (the only thing left over from my ever so tasty ice cream), and got in line. Shuffling along the aisle with all the other passengers, my seat of choice was in sight. I like to sit on the right side of the plane two rows behind the wing. Pretty silly, right? You're thinking, *Just take a seat—any seat.*

Little did I know that on this particular day, there would be a reason for me to be seated in Row 17, Seat A. Tired from speaking at a weekend retreat, this would be a great time for me to rest before arriving home to my family. Arranging my pink floral bag under the seat in front of me, placing a blanket over my legs, I was ready for a nap.

**FYI**—A tip on plane etiquette. Anytime one is covered up or has a book out . . . that means, don't interrupt.

Anyway, that's exactly when it happened. The tattoo girl headed straight for the seat between the bearded man and me. As she approached the aisle, she made eye contact with me. My thought was correct. Not only was she taking the middle seat, which would crowd me, she had a very large backpack, which she stuffed under the seat in front of her and then plopped her feet on top of

*A tip on plane etiquette:*

*Anytime one is*

*covered up or has a*

*book out . . . that means,*

*don't interrupt.*

it. Then much to my surprise she turned to me, stuck out her hand, and with a smile that brightened her face, she said, "Hi, I'm Madison."

You won't believe what happened next.

She said, "You're a believer, right?

"Aaaa believer in what?" I curiously responded.

"A Christ follower?" she said.

Somewhat in shock I quickly responded, "Well, yes, I am."

"I knew it," she said. "We have something to celebrate. I just shared Jesus with that girl (pointing a few rows ahead of us), and we now have a new sister in Christ!" Putting her hand in the air awaiting a high five, I gave it to her.

OK . . . OK . . . just imagine the look on my face. Better yet, just imagine the one on God's. I felt terrible for what I had assumed about this girl at first glance. The Holy Spirit quickly reminded me of the message God told Samuel. (*"Looks aren't everything. Don't be impressed with his looks and stature. . . . God judges persons differently than humans do. Men and women look at the face; God looks into the heart"* —1 Samuel 16:7 The Message.)

The conversation lasted the entire trip. While she was talking, I was thinking how God has such a great sense of humor. You see, before getting on the flight I told the Lord I didn't want to talk to anyone on this flight because I was too tired from ministering all weekend. No problem. He took care of that for me. God sat her down right where He needed her to be; ministering to Chandra Peele. I sat speechless (doesn't happen very often) as she shared her story. The tattoos were from her past life, before she met Jesus Christ.

Her birth mother was a drug addict, and since age 3, Madison had been tossed from foster family to foster family. When Madison was 16, feeling unloved and out of place, she began to look for love in all the wrong places. Trying to find her place in this world, Madison had become friends with a guy whose dad was a body artist. Unfortunately Madison volunteered to be his guinea pig.

In the midst of that year something miraculous happened. Her biological grandmother found her and took her home. Her eyes filled with tears of joy when she told me about the day her 63-year-old grandmother looked passed all the tattoos and loved her with an agape love. It wasn't too long before her grandmother's love for Jesus spilled over onto her. "My grandmother had one request; that I would go to church with her every Sunday," she explained to me.

Madison went on to share how she had never gone to church but it didn't take long for her to become interested in this man named Jesus. Madison gave her life to Jesus Christ, and she began to notice a change on the inside. She stretched out her arm and showed me a tattoo on her forearm that really bothered her more than any of the others. It was a dragon, and she felt that it was somewhat demonic looking. She wanted it removed, so her grandmother gave her the money for the removal. Unfortunately the pain was unbearable, so instead of removing it, they added a new tattoo. It was a cross with a red banner and the name of Jesus draped across it.

She said that day she experienced many emotions. The pain she endured that day reminded her of her painful past. The tears of sadness came from repentance of bad choices. And tears of joy were shed as she embraced the hope she now has in Jesus. Peace fills her heart and from that day forward she prays that her life will illuminate God's love so bright that people will see past the tattoos like her grandmother did.

She told me that some of the people in the church were very kind to her but others looked at her with judgmental eyes. Of course my heart was breaking knowing I had just been one of those "church people" who stamped her with DEFECT before ever giving her a chance. I was so ashamed. "Lord, forgive me for judging my sister," I silently prayed.

Madison had a burning desire to share her story of being lost and how she has now found Jesus with anyone who would listen. "I am so thankful, and when I share my story it's like thanking God every time," she beamed.

One church wouldn't let her work with their youth. Another church leader told her that she should wear dresses that would conceal her tattoos when coming to church. I wanted to hug her tight and tell her I was sorry for all the Christians in the universe who had hurt her. She said, "God loves me unconditionally, and that's all that really matters."

Amazingly, she didn't let the stares and the whispers hurt her. Instead through the Word and power of the Holy Spirit she gained a new confidence. She made herself available and she heard the Lord say, "Follow Me." At 21 she travels the United States sharing the gospel of Jesus Christ.

**Open your Bible and read Mark 16:15.**

*Go into all the world and preach the good news to all creation. Whoever believes and is baptized will be saved, but whoever does not believe will be condemned.*

This young Christian sister taught me so much. Her story greatly impacted my life. Talk about a wake up call! It is clear to me that the Lord needed to adjust my spiritual eyesight. Madison was truly transformed from the inside out.

Isn't it great to know there is no cookie cutter for Christians? No specific race, color, shape, fashion style, fancy hat, Bible size, or hairstyle. Each child of God is unique.

**Open your Bible and read Psalm 139:14.**

*Body and soul, I am marvelously made!*
*(The Message).*

## The Power of Perception

Perception is the basis for our assumptions about others and us. When we take ownership of our own perceptions, we must also realize that others may or may not have the same perception. As Christians we need to be aware of our perceptions toward others.

Perception is influenced by:
  a. physical characteristics
  b. personality
  c. gender, social, cultural identities

*The definition of perception—process of assigning meaning to sensory information and experiences.*

Have you formed an opinion about someone before you took the time to get to know her? Maybe your perception of her was because of the color of her skin, the kind of hairstyle she had, or maybe the clothes she wore.

Take a moment to pray. Ask God to give you a new perspective to see with spiritual eyes. Write your prayer here.

_____

_____

_____

_____

_____

_____

_____

Imagine the godly influence we can be by showing unconditional love to a person we have wrongly judged. We can admit our actions and God will begin to change our hearts. When we have a growing relationship with the Father, He tenderly begins to reveal our ungodly attitudes. When we see with His eyes, we often have a new perception.

God had given Madison's grandmother a godly perspective. When she met Madison, she didn't cringe at the site of her face piercings or her tattoos. God's love for Madison was greater than any love she had ever known. He sent her grandmother after all these years to show her His perfect love. This love changed her life! She was transformed! Now today she illuminates His love to others. Her light shines brightly to all those who meet her. God loves us all. He can give us all a light that shines brightly for Him.

**Ask yourself these questions:**
- Has God sent someone into your life to help you recognize:
    His love?
    His truth?
    His forgiveness?
    His grace?
- Be careful not to be judgmental of others or legalistic in words and direction.
- The best way to show others Christ is by example. What or whom does your life reflect?

Jesus said, *"Do not judge others, and you will not be judged. For you will be treated as you treat others. The standard you use in judging is the standard by which you are judged"* (Matthew 7:1–2 NLT)

We have to be careful to speak the truth in love. As Christians we teach others by our love.

## My Father's Eyes

Today as I lay under this old oak tree . . . must be more than 100 years old . . . I can't help but take my eyes off all that surrounds me in this big open space. These huge branches hang to the ground, resembling an umbrella. I see a bright blue sky peeking through each leaf and bare branch. Then my focus comes closer as I notice the tiny red ladybug crawling on a bright green leaf. I can't help but see God's hand in it all, as I know heaven is above

*An authentic fun-loving Christian—one who radiates God's love is far more effective than a Christian who is rigid, judgmental, and legalistic.*

that which I can see. My glance keeps coming back to the branches of this big ol' tree. It's huge! The carving in the trunk; the ants crawling in a straight line up the trunk into a whole so tiny, but oh so deep, to the moss that clings to every other branch. It's all unique. It's all created by the One who created me.

Then lying so still, trying my best not to even blink my eyes, I watch two redbirds on the branch just above my head. The color red is so brilliant as it rests against the green leaf. Listening to the whistle, the beautiful music that comes from these tiny little birds, I feel a gentle breeze as it blows against my face. It's as though I feel the breath of God in the stillness of this divine moment. Wait. I think my vision is becoming clearer. Could this be how God sees His creation? Is this what I am missing every day? The simple things? Creation?

In that moment my prayer is a humble cry to God. Wiping the tear that has rolled down the side of my face near my ear I pray, "Oh, God, that I could be still more often. That I might see Your creation as You see it more often. That my eyes would be opened to see people like I see Your beauty in the creation You have placed all around me. Change my heart through my eyes, Lord. Help me to see as You see."

Leaving the ranch and getting back to my normal space, I realize the Lord is answering my prayer. I can't take my eyes off of people.

They are fascinating! Every move, every statement, every cry from a baby, each responsive act catches my glance. In this moment my eyes are off me and focused on others.

Today, more than any other day, I feel like I can

love. I can see into the hearts of the people around me, people at the grocery store and the mall, the woman behind the counter, the beggar on the street corner, the little girl riding her bike down the block, the neighbor pulling weeds from her garden. Could it be that this is just a glimpse of the unconditional love that God has for me? I wonder just how many of these people who so desperately need love have never experienced the sweet love of God. With these new eyes I have a desire to show others His love.

God gave me a glimpse of more than human vision. He gave me agape vision. From the beggar on the street corner with dark teeth and dirty clothes, to the new employee nervously messing up behind the counter, I can now see them in a different way. To the seemingly perfect high school girl walking past me looking great but staring through the crowd with empty eyes, to the widow who is lonely, the sick who just need to be heard, the poor who need a helping hand, the child who just needs someone to listen, with my new eyes I can see that God loves them all.

*What would it be like to have a different vision?* I wonder, *to step out into the world each day with eyes wide open ready to see what God the Creator has set into motion.* I would love more. I would laugh more. I would serve more. I would rest more. I would give more. I would glorify God more!

Oh, Lord, give me new vision. In each moment give me grace to see, a heart that is opened, and a joy that not only brings new light to my eyes, but that spreads like fire to those around me.

Oh, Lord, that I could have my Father's eyes.

## The Carrot

Here's a test. Let's look at a carrot. What color is it? When we cut the carrot into slices, what color is it? When we blend it and make it into juice, what color is it? Can we say ORANGE?

Are we like carrots? What you see is what you get, or do you change with the crowd like a chameleon? In other words, are you a Christian through and through? Do your friends know the real you?

## The Kiwi

Here's a quiz: What's brown and fuzzy on the outside, and green and beautiful on the inside?

Whether we like kiwi or not, we have to agree it's green, juicy, and beautiful inside! I wonder how long it took before someone finally decided to cut open the brown, fuzzy fruit. Can you imagine the surprise when they discovered its inner beauty and sweetness?

Maybe some of us have a personality like the kiwi. We're the shy, sensitive type that most people never get to know. Or, maybe like the kiwi we don't feel pretty on the outside. We don't stand out like the carrot. We're not as confident as the carrot. If people were able to see the real us from the inside out, what would they see? Are there some things we wish people could see and know about the real us?

What would we want others to see that perhaps they don't?

What does God see when He looks at our hearts?

*Have you ever had thoughts like this running through your mind?*

# Get Real!

Take a close look at yourself. Do you pretend to be a good Christian in front of a crowd or are you really a Christian through and through?

_____

When looking at yourself, what is your perception?

_____

Do you think others have a good perception of you?

_____

Have you changed after giving your life to Jesus? What differences have you noticed?

_____

What evidence is there of "New Life" in you?

_____

_____

Are there areas in your life that you have not turned over to God?

_____

_____

Have you ever had thoughts like this running through your mind?

"OK, God, You're great and all, but I just want You to stay in charge of this part of my life. I can handle the rest on my own."

Be specific and describe on what occasion or in which area of your life you have these thoughts. Write your response.

_____

_____

_____

_____

We need to be honest with ourselves and admit areas of weakness. Sometimes we can get so good at faking it that we fool ourselves. Coming face-to-face with our sins or perhaps our selfish pride isn't fun. However, it can be a time of spiritual growth. Just remember that God loves us so much, and He's not finished with us yet. We're a work in progress. Just like Madison. Just like me. Just like everyone!

Reflect on the following and then write your response on the lines below.

I have left God out of a particular area of my life. I admit wanting to be in charge when it comes to . . .

_____

_____

_____

_____

_____

_____

_____

_____

_____

_____

_____

# GAB Session
## ~~ with Chandra ~~

Several years ago my husband, Bruce, and I held a Bible study in our home for students. On one particular night after a time of worship and praise, we studied the story of Nicodemus. After our study I asked if anyone in the room would like to share their personal testimony when they were "born again." It became a wonderful night of sharing as many of the students shared their stories. What happened next was so exciting and such an example of God's power when we talk about Him to others.

Two girls had tears streaming down their beautiful faces. One of them begin to share that she had been going to church with her friends for many years and during the testimonies she realized she had never asked Christ to be her Savior. Several other students began to share verses in the Bible. Through the power of Christ and the testimonies of others, these two girls left my house different that night. They each prayed and invited Jesus to be their Lord and Savior. They were "new" in Christ that night.

We need each other for encouragement and support. Together we can read the Word and attend church to learn more about how to be radiant for Him. We can stop right now, and pray for our brothers and sisters who do not know Jesus as their personal Savior and Lord. We can pray for ourselves too. We can invite Jesus into our hearts. Let's pray right now.

The Transformation

**Warning!** Satan wants to steal your joy. He wants you to have doubts about everything you have learned in this study. Don't let him win. He is a loser! Jesus Christ is victorious over all. Call out to Him and He will answer you. Remember you can lose everything—all your belongings, your friends, your family, your material possessions—but you can never lose Jesus. He will be with you always. He will never leave you. (*Trust Him; believe His promises; and give each day to Him. God is in control! Love to you and may God bless you immeasurably more than you can even imagine* —Ephesians 3:20.)

*Warning! Satan wants to steal your joy.*

# My Journal

Write your testimony starting with at least one sentence talking about the time before you committed your life to Jesus. Include where you were when you made this commitment, the name of the person you were with if anyone, and how you felt that day. If you know the date, you can include that too. Close out your testimony by sharing how Jesus has transformed your life and what He has done for you. Praise God for all the things He has done to transform you.

# My Journal

# My Journal

# My Journal

# My Journal

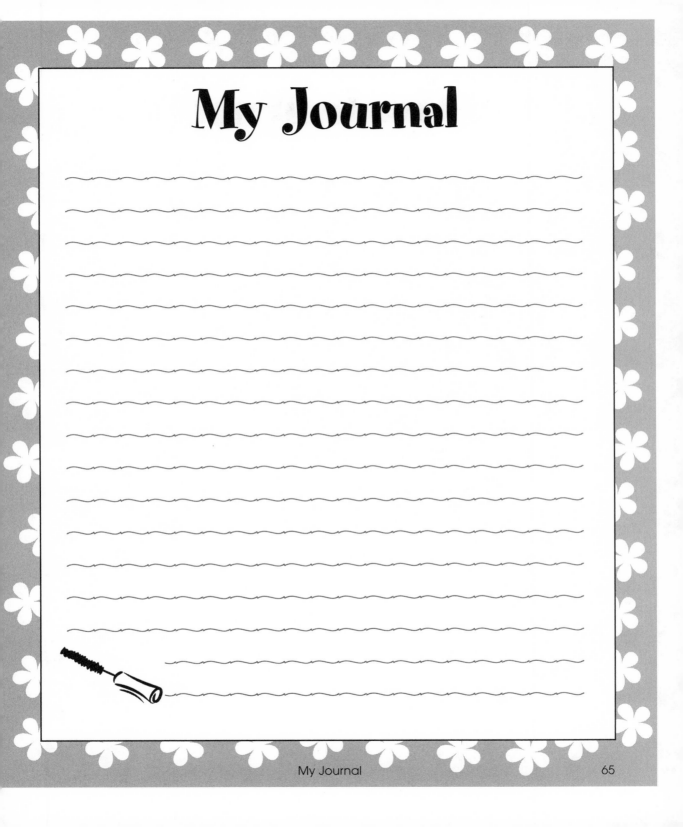

# My Journal

s e s s i o n   3

# The Real YOU!

Each of us is a princess, a child of the King. Not just any king but the King of kings. God knew us and shaped us in our mothers' wombs. He knows everything about us. He knows the beat of our hearts, the number of hairs on our heads, what makes us happy and sad. He knows what we think and how we feel. He's there with us in our secret places, and He cares about our every need and thought. He loves us with an everlasting love. He thinks we are all beautiful because each of us is His special child.

Although you may be older now, are there still times when you dream of being held? God is our heavenly Father. We can always crawl up into His lap and let Him hold us. We can tell Him everything, our fears, hurts, doubts, and pain. We can share our deepest thoughts with Him, our desires, our needs, and our dreams. He wants to hear it all. He longs to have these intimate moments with us.

Jesus wants to:

- be our true love
- be first in our lives
- bless us with abundant life
- provide for us more than we could ever imagine

When we forget who we are, we can remember Whose we are.

The Real YOU!                                                          67

## Read the following out loud. Then mark these verses in your Bible.

I am . . .

A child of God (Romans 8:16)

Forgiven (Colossians 1:13–14)

Kept in safety wherever I go (Psalm 91:10–11)

Delivered from the power of darkness (Colossians 1:13)

Victorious (Revelation 21:7)

Free from condemnation (Romans 8:1)

An heir of eternal life (1 John 5:11–12)

More than a conqueror (Romans 8:37)

Firmly rooted, built up, strengthened in my faith
(Colossians 2:7)

An ambassador for Christ (2 Corinthians 5:20)

One in Christ (John 17:21–23)

Christ's friend (John 15:15)

A daughter of light not of darkness (1 Thessalonians 5:5)

Fearfully and wonderfully made (Psalm 139:14)

I am the daughter of the King.

You can believe that you are to die for. And how do you know this?

### Open your Bible and read John 3:16.

*For God so loved the world that He gave His one and only Son, that whoever believed in him shall not perish but have eternal life.*

*You can believe*

*that you are to die for.*

*And how do you*

*know this?*

# The Story of God's Precious Princess

Once upon a time there was a little girl, and she was the apple of her father's eye. He loved her more than anything. In fact, all he did was care about her every thought, her every move, her every desire. He had a pedestal that he sat her upon and when she was up on that stool, nothing could distract her because she couldn't take her eyes off her father. Eye to eye, heart to heart, they would talk about everything. She would tell her daddy how wonderful he was and that there could never be another above him. He would always reply, "My precious princess, I love you."

She would tell her daddy she loved him every day, many times, because she knew how much he loved hearing those words, and she wanted to please him more than anything. Although they had many happy, fun, and joyous times together, there were also times when she needed her father's advice or help. Sometimes she would be hurt or scared. She knew he would be waiting, longing for her to tell him every detail. She would run to him, and he would pick her up. As he carried her and held her close, the tears in her eyes seemed to turn into tears of joy. Mysteriously, the hurt seemed to fall to the floor and melt away. She always skipped after she left him because she felt such peace and freedom.

Sometimes the little girl would make bad choices and run to her father, knowing he would be disappointed. To her amazement, even then he reached out his arms to hold her. She would ask for his thoughts and tuck each word of wisdom into her heart.

"My precious princess, you are becoming more and more like me each day we spend together. I can see a reflection of me when I look at you. Others are talking about our resemblance. Nothing blesses me more. Know that I will never leave you. I will always be here for you. When you grow up and have another love in your life, always keep me first. Keep talking with me and telling me every need you have, because nothing pleases me more than to care and watch over you. You are my precious princess, and I love you."

The little girl grew up and moved away. She missed her daddy so much, but every day she opened their special book and read the love letters he had written for her. It seemed as if he always knew what she needed for that moment. She was comforted that even though he wasn't where she could see him, he was there in her heart.

One day the girl became ill and her father came to visit. When she saw him, she reached out to him and said, "Oh, Daddy, take me home."

He took her hand and led her to the home he had prepared for her. She was in awe of what her father had done and bowed down before him. "Daddy!" she exclaimed. "It's so good to be home." And together they lived happily forever and ever and ever.

Isn't it great to know there is no "The End" to this story?

Just like this little girl, we have a father. In fact, you have two fathers, an earthly father and a heavenly Father. Each of us has a different story about our earthly father. Some of us are blessed with the sweetest, kindest daddies, while others may have fathers that don't know Jesus and are less than we had hoped for in a daddy. Some of us may have never even met our fathers.

Let's talk about those who may have never met their fathers. It must be so hard to see God as a Father if we don't have a father to compare Him with. Let's imagine for a moment the father of our dreams. Then imagine that all of those dreams come true and that he is even better than what we expected. This is how God, the Father, loves us. He loves us individually. His love for us is never-ending. He loves for us to talk to Him and share our thoughts and needs with Him. He is never too busy. When we call on Him, we will never get a busy signal or a "leave a message after the beep." We'll never hear Him say, "I'll get back with you when I have time."

We can experience this perfect love as we grow in our relationship with Him. God, the Father, can be "your everything." Whatever our story is, if we know the heavenly Father, we can have this kind of relationship like the little girl had with her daddy in the story.

Have you spent some special times alone with God, the Father, just you and Him? Do you like to get in His lap and tell Him everything? Why don't you take some time to do that now?

**Open your Bible and read Psalm 46:10.**
Write what this verse means to you.

_____

_____

_____

_____

_____

When you are close to God, can you feel His loving arms holding you? Write about a time when you ran to Him with tears of pain and He picked you up and carried you through the storm.

_____

_____

_____

_____

_____

Did you grow closer to the Father because of the experience? Write about this time, and share it with a friend. (It might just be that God wants to use your story to bring someone else closer to Him.)

_____

_____

_____

_____

_____

Has there been a time when God used someone else's story to speak to you?

Do you notice when others have a close walk with God? What about you? How are you and Jesus today? Get real with yourself. Be honest.

## Meditate on Psalm 45:10-11.

*Listen, O daughter, consider and give ear: Forget your people and your father's house. The king is enthralled by your beauty; honor him, for he is your lord.*

## Read this prayer out loud.

*Dear Lord,*
*I know that You love when I run to You, when I talk to You about every detail of my life. You really do care more than anyone else. You care about the little things, the silly things, and even the dumb things. Lord, I pray that You will continue to pursue me, and that I will hear You when You call my name. It is my desire to have an intimate relationship with You. Forgive me, Lord, when I put my selfish wants before You. Forgive me for running to others before I run to You. I love You, Father.*
*Amen.*

# My Journal

Write the answer to this question: What are your thoughts when you consider yourself a princess, a precious child of the King?

# My Journal

# My Journal

_____

_____

_____

_____

_____

_____

_____

_____

_____

_____

_____

_____

_____

_____

_____

# My Journal

# My Journal

# Heir to the King

*Now if we are children, then we are heirs—heirs of God and co-heirs with Christ, if indeed we share in his sufferings in order that we may also share in his glory.*
—Romans 8:17

Princess. Even the word is beautiful! OK, let's think back to when we were little girls, playing dress up, pretending to be a beautiful princess, playing in Mom's closet putting on high heels and a pretty dress, or maybe even her lipstick. Most of us loved this time. Those days as a little child were simple, silly, and so fun! And then we grew up.

## Project Princess

Do you have a favorite princess? Is she a fairy-tale princess or the real deal?
What characteristic or quality makes her stand out to you? Write your response below.

_____

_____

_____

*Project Princess*

_____

_____

_____

What are your thoughts when you consider the character and beauty of a princess?

There is no correct answer, just your thoughts and opinions. Write yours here.

_____

_____

_____

_____

## The Crown Jewels

The Tower of London houses the crown jewels, and they have been displayed for public viewing since the seventeenth century. These jewels have great value and are polished and dusted before viewing every year at the royal coronation of the monarchs of the United Kingdom.

In addition to their historic value, the crown jewels include several spectacular and priceless gems. Imagine the size of the most valuable stone, which is the First Star of Africa. This stone weighs just over 530 carats.

What does this have to do with our being princesses? Although these precious stones are considered priceless gems to the world, we are priceless gems to God, our heavenly Father. The world makes such a fuss over jewels, gold, money, cars, houses, and clothes, but none of it matters when it comes to eternity. We can't take anything with us to heaven, and even if we could, the jewels that we held in our hands wouldn't be worth anything. We would be the jewel walking through the pearly gates of heaven. Isn't it awesome to think we are more valuable to God than the most precious of all the jewels in the world?

**Open your Bible and read 1 Corinthians 9:25.**
What does the verse say to you? Write your response below.

_____

_____

_____

_____

_____

Paul gives a great example of one who runs a race to win the crown. He practices, prepares, and trains; however, the crown he is racing for has no value in heaven.

Have you ever gone to someone's house and seen tons of trophies on shelves? I have. I felt worthless because I have never received a trophy. I left feeling sorry for myself, or maybe a better way to describe my feeling was that I felt a need to prove myself. Isn't that silly?

In the world, trophies build up people, but in heaven they are worthless. As Christians, we must run a different kind of race. Prayer, Bible study, and worship equip us to run with zeal and vigor. Our spiritual growth depends on it. We should be prepared, deny ourselves, and make our goals to please God. The trophy we receive is eternal and it's a crown that will last forever.

When living life and running the race to please our heavenly Father, we need to be encouraged. When it seems we are falling behind, remember, we've got the power! The power of the Holy Spirit that lives within each of us.

Through Christ all things are possible. But the Bible also says in Revelation, that when we get to heaven, we will lay our crowns at the feet of Jesus. We won't even want them. Only He is worthy of praise!

For those who understand this message, there is incredible freedom, forgiveness, and new life in Christ Jesus.

**Have you ever come in first place in a race? Describe your feelings below.**

_____

_____

_____

_____

_____

If you're not a runner or can't remember running anytime recently, think back to your elementary school days. Did you have something called "field day"? Whether you came in first or last, reflect back on the race and write about it.

_____

_____

*Have you ever come in first place in a race?*

You may have been a winner, or maybe you tripped on the starting line and all you remember is skinning your knees in front of all your friends. Whatever your story, always know that when running the race as a Christian, God is running with you. When you trip and fall or lag behind in last place, trust Jesus to pick you up and carry you to the finish line. With Jesus, you are promised to win the prize, the crown of life. Now that's a trophy everyone can receive.

Here are some questions for you to think about. Reflect on your answers and pray about your needs. You may not be actually running a race, but you are running the race of life.

- How are you in the race of life right now?
- Are you in first?
- Are you lagging behind huffing and puffing?
- Have you tripped and not been able to get up?
- Have people on the sidelines caused you to feel embarrassed or not worthy of running the race?
- Have you decided there is no reason to continue?
- Do you feel like a failure? Why or why not?
- Do you have someone running with you? Who? How does this person help or hinder?

*When running the race as a Christian, God is running with you.*

- Are you greatly supported and encouraged or feel that you're in the race alone?
- Do you have confidence that you will finish? From where does your confidence come?

## The Royal Clothing

*For he has clothed me with garments of salvation and arrayed me in a robe of righteousness.*
—Isaiah 61:10–11.

When we belong to God, we also are co-heirs with Jesus, His Son. We are clothed in His righteousness. From rags to riches is a true statement here.

**Open your Bible and read Isaiah 64:6.**
What does this verse say to you? Write your response below.

_____

_____

_____

_____

_____

_____

_____

Meditate on the verse before reading further.

We put so much effort into what we wear. Again, it is freeing to know that nothing we wear or don't wear is going to make a difference in how God looks at us. Yes, we need to reflect Christ in our modest dress, but really, even that requires a right heart, not a logo or brand.

In the movie *The Princess Diaries*, a makeover is what it took to change the character Mia into a beautiful princess. Do you sometimes think that if only you had a personal hairdresser and makeup artist at your house every day, maybe you would look like a princess? Well, the truth is, you already do. If it takes a prince coming to you and swooping you off your feet to make you a princess, He's already extended the invitation to you. He thinks you are the most beautiful of all. Oh? Who is that Prince? He is Jesus.

True beauty comes from the inside out. Who are we on the inside? Once we can overcome the world and its sinful ways, then we can begin to see through the make-up and the clothes and all the things that can often cover up our true beauty. Read His love letters and believe His promises. Only then will we see that we are royalty!

Write a letter as if God, the heavenly Father, were writing to you. What do you think He would say to you? Remember He sees your heart.

_____

_____

_____

_____

_____

*True beauty comes from the inside out.*

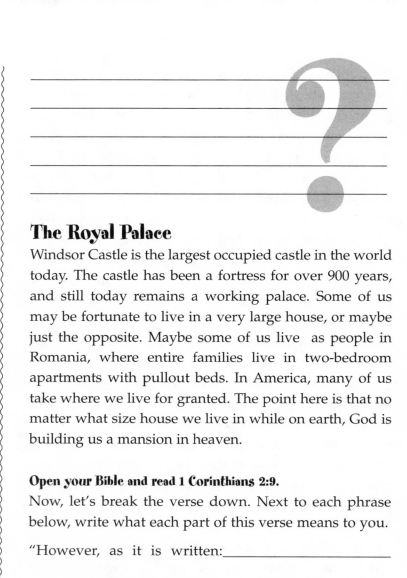

_____
_____
_____
_____
_____

## The Royal Palace

Windsor Castle is the largest occupied castle in the world today. The castle has been a fortress for over 900 years, and still today remains a working palace. Some of us may be fortunate to live in a very large house, or maybe just the opposite. Maybe some of us live as people in Romania, where entire families live in two-bedroom apartments with pullout beds. In America, many of us take where we live for granted. The point here is that no matter what size house we live in while on earth, God is building us a mansion in heaven.

**Open your Bible and read 1 Corinthians 2:9.**

Now, let's break the verse down. Next to each phrase below, write what each part of this verse means to you.

"However, as it is written:_____

_____

"'No eye has seen, no ear has heard, no mind has conceived what God has prepared for those who love him'

_____

"but God has revealed it to us by his Spirit."_____

_____

As magnificent as Windsor Castle is, it can't begin to compare to our home in heaven. God, our heavenly Father, loves us so much that He wants us to know life here on earth is temporary. He reminds us that we shouldn't get all caught up in earthly pleasures because nothing can compare to what He has prepared for us who love Him. Isn't that exciting?

No matter how much we love our earthly fathers, they can never be our everything. It is so important for us to know God, the Father, personally and intimately because the day may come when we have to let our earthly daddies go. Let me explain.

I was blessed with a wonderful, godly father who loved me very much. Not only did he love me, he provided for me, gave me boundaries, and was a great example for me. So when I sat beside my father's bed as he was walking through the valley of the shadow of death, it was a difficult time.

This particular day will be in my memory forever. I was reading to him, and he reached out his hand and told me to be quiet. I said, "Oh, Daddy, I'm sorry; do you not want me to read to you?"

He responded, "Yes, just a minute."

My daddy, lying flat on his back, sick and weak with the cancer that filled his body smiled as he looked up to someone I could not see and said, "Hi, how are you?" The conversation continued and went something like this.

"How are you?" Daddy said to the invisible person above him. "Good. OK. About four o'clock. OK, I'll be ready. OK, bye."

Although I couldn't hear the other side of the conversation, I somehow knew what was being said. The person left and my daddy turned to me smiling and said, "That was that sweet woman that was with me in surgery. She said my new home is ready for me." Then he smiled even bigger and said, "She's going with me when I go."

I never questioned Daddy about the four o'clock, but I just had a feeling that would be the time the Lord would take him home. And He did. My daddy took his last breath just before four o'clock the next Saturday afternoon.

During this time I realized the importance of my daddy not just being my father but also my brother in God's family. It wasn't his identity of being my father that gave him the assurance of eternal life, but it was that he is my brother, co-heirs with Jesus Christ that gave him this assurance. That is also what gave me peace, and strangely, even joy when he took his last breath. Someday I'll see my daddy again! (*"For where your treasure is, there your heart will be also"* —Matthew 6:21.)

Our treasure cannot be bought. We find our treasures when we come to know Jesus as Lord of our lives. And those treasures we discover will cause us to be radiant in Him.

Wow! When I realize how much God, the Father, has waiting for me in heaven, it sure gives me the freedom and hope to live this life on earth. It changes everything. My focus is upward. I realize my purpose is so much greater than the petty, silly things in which I have put so much energy. Sharing what God has done in my life is exciting! I used to be so concerned with my house and material things before I realized it took my focus off of God and put it on me. Me. Me. Me! It was all about me!

**Read this prayer and then spend time listening to what God is saying to you.**

*Thank You, God, for getting my attention. I place my focus on You and You alone. I'm weak but You are strong. Lord, You are the treasure that I seek. When I am faithful to seek You first, my heart is filled with joy on the good days and even on the really, really bad days. Oh, God, may I be radiant for You in all I do and say. Amen.*

# GAB Session
## ~ with Chandra ~

At a retreat with a group of moms and daughters we were discussing what it means to consider ourselves daughters of the King. We talked about Princess Dianna and how so many people looked up to her. We also recognized that everywhere she went, whether in a beautiful, one-of-a-kind, gorgeous formal gown or in a pair of jeans hanging out with her sons, she was beautiful. She wore wonderful one-of-a-kind designer clothing, lived in a castle, did good things for others, was called the Princess of the People, but that none of it really mattered in the end.

We know she didn't need her earthly crown when she entered heaven. All she needed was Jesus.
Now we may not have a banner across our bodies that label us as a princess, but that's OK. We don't need one. Our King loves us just the way we are. He created us, and we are His masterpiece. The day we committed our lives to Him, He gave us a makeover. He made us a new creation and we bring glory and honor to our Father, the King.

In Revelation 4:10–11 the Bible says that we will give our crowns to Him.

> *They lay their crowns before the throne and say: You are worthy, our Lord and our God, to receive glory and honor and power, for you created all things, and by your will they were created.*

We are joint heirs with Jesus, the Son of God. We are royalty!

# My Journal

What are your thoughts when you consider yourself a princess of the King? For extra study on the family of God, read 1 John 5:18-21. What does this Scripture say to you?

# My Journal

# My Journal

_____

_____

_____

_____

_____

_____

_____

_____

_____

_____

_____

_____

_____

_____

# My Journal

# My Journal

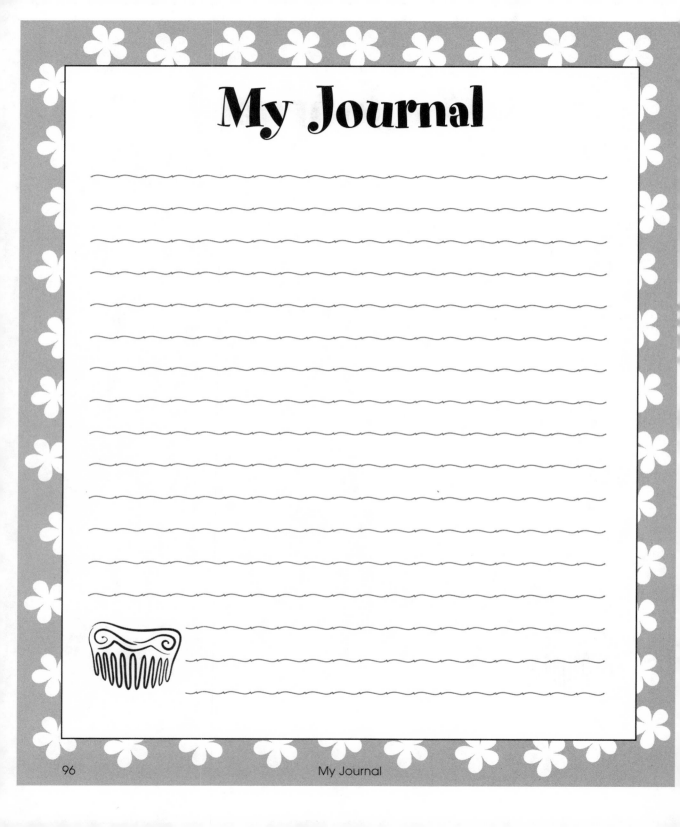

# The Beauty and the Beast in Me

**W**hy is it that we are so negative about ourselves? How can we look in the mirror and find the one little zit on our faces and wammo! Our day is ruined! And usually it's not just one day, but also the next three days. When we look at ourselves in the mirror, our eyes go right to it. It bugs us. We feel ugly and think everyone else is looking at it too.

Let's talk about what others really see. Of course, people see our outer appearances, and for first impressions, sadly enough, outer appearances are very important to most people. In time, we look past the outer appearances and see others for who they really are. We like people who are happy, fun, encouraging, helpful, or most importantly, authentic. REAL! Let's stop right here for a minute and do an exercise.

*In time, we look past the outer appearances and see others for who they really are.*

# Think About the Following Questions.

- Why have you chosen the friends you have?
- Do you agree that "true beauty" can only come from within a person? Why?

If we are godly, then we can't help but bloom into beautiful people. Everything beautiful about us is because of the spirit of Jesus living in us. Through this intimate relationship with God, the Father, we can actually like who we are. Without Him, we're empty. With Him, we are full. We realize that everything "special" about us is a gift from Him. That attitude comes only from the heart of a person, and that, my friend, is true beauty.

When you are positive about yourself, chances are great that your relationship with God is good. When you haven't been with God, haven't read the Bible, haven't been with other Christians, or haven't been obedient, chances are you don't like yourself or anyone else for that mater.

Get a mirror. What do you see when you look into the mirror? See past the hair, makeup, glasses, nose, cheeks, chin, eyebrows, mouth, and teeth. Look deep inside. Look way down inside, all the way to your heart. After you do this, what do you think? Do you like what you see? Are there some changes you should make? Do you like who you are?

Girls have told me before that no one really knows them. After reading these pages, maybe you will want others to know the real you.

You may need to stop here for a minute or maybe longer to really determine who you are. When you shift your identity to be more like Jesus, then you can be

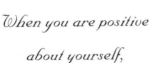

*When you are positive about yourself, chances are great that your relationship with God is good.*

assured to like who and what you see. Others will notice a difference too.

Try this. In the morning right when you wake up say, "Good morning, Lord." Then stand in front of the mirror and say, "Lord, here I am. I empty myself of me. (Envision your body being like a bathtub with a drain at the bottom. Now pull the plug and let all of you drain out.) Lord, I ask that You would fill me up with Your living water so high that I am running over. Lord, I want to be a bright light, a reflection of You everywhere I go today. Lord, I want to glorify You today so I ask for opportunities in my path so others will see You in me.

Thank You, Jesus!"

**The World would say . . .**
**Mirror, mirror on the wall,**
**Who's the fairest of them all?**
**Daughters of the King would say . . .**
**Mirror, mirror on the wall,**
**Do you see Jesus in me at all?**

Print this and put it on your mirror to remind you that you belong to Him.

When we learn to do this, we will have more confidence in who we are in Christ. We will also come to understand God's supernatural power; another word for glory is *power*. Once we have invited the Lord to fill us with His glory, we also receive His power. How awesome is that? God wants us to be passionate about our relationship with Him. Our enthusiasm will draw others to Him. When we take the focus off ourselves and put it on Jesus, we'll see things differently. We become OK with who we are and how we look. Now we can see others differently because of God's love and power in us.

A simple of definition of *self-esteem* is the value we attach to our self-concept. We read in 1 Peter 3:3–4, *"Your beauty should not come from outward adornment, such as braided hair and wearing of gold jewelry and fine clothes. Instead, it should be that of your inner self, the unfading beauty of a gentle and quiet spirit, which is of great worth in God's sight."*

Peter is not telling us specifically "Don't braid your hair and don't wear gold jewelry." He instead wants us to notice that we seem to put too high a priority on the clothes we wear, the brand of purse we carry, or the car we drive. We do these things to please people, to fit in, and to fulfill our selfish desires, rather than to please God. It sounds funny that people can worship clothing and other material things, but it's true. We should worship the Lord, our God, and Him alone. He alone is worthy of our worship.

# GAB Session
## ~ with Chandra ~

Shopping is fun, and I must admit, I really like clothes. And nothing is wrong with shopping unless it gets out of control. Cute trendy clothes entice me when in the store, so sometimes I charge them on my credit card. What I fail to consider is the debt I'll have when the bill comes.

God calls us to be good stewards with what He has given us. We all should know our financial limit. As young women shopping on our own, regardless if it's our money or Mom's credit card, consider a budget. If we are blessed with plenty of money, and we are giving a portion to the Lord and to others, then our limit is between us and our parents and the Lord. We must each ask ourselves, "Am I being a good steward with what God has given me?"

When there are no boundaries and we lack self-control, we can get into trouble.

I have done the silliest things when it comes to buying clothes. I have spent a lot of money on one outfit that I thought I just had to have and wore it only two or three times. Now it hangs in my closet collecting dust. What was I thinking? Have I become obsessed with what I wear? Have I become materialistic?

*Prayer: Oh, God, once again I need Your help. Remind me, Lord, that everything I have is a gift from You. Help me to be a good steward of all You have given me.*

# Standing Out in a Crowd

Sometimes we see people who really are, shall we say, definitely different. Perhaps they have chosen to dress in really revealing or really tight clothes or maybe they wear lots of jewelry on unique places on their bodies. We immediately start to stare because they stand out in the crowd. Maybe they just need this kind of attention to feel good about themselves. Of course, there is nothing wrong with being unique in how we dress, but we know the difference in unique and inappropriate. What Peter is talking about in his letter is that we can wear things that bring honor to God and not attention to ourselves.

Peter is helping us see how caught up we can get in clothing and style. He is teaching us that the condition of our hearts is what is really important to God. This is true beauty that comes from the inside. All that outward adornment can be a cover-up of what's really going on inside a person, the mask we hide behind. Think about it. If our bodies are temples of the Holy Spirit, what we wear should be a reflection of Christ. Keeping our dress moral doesn't mean we have to wear long skirts, sweaters, and a cover over our heads. We can still dress fun, trendy, and in style. Keeping a high standard of dress is a challenge, but we'll be rewarded for honoring God in the way we dress. This is a perfect example of dying to self to live for Christ.

**Open your Bible and read 2 Corinthians 3:18.**

*But we all, with unveiled face, beholding as in a mirror the glory of the Lord, are being transformed into the same image from glory to glory, just as by the spirit of the Lord (NKJV).*

Take a close look at the clothes in your closet. Do you have more clothes than you can actually wear? Maybe some of the clothes need to be given to a clothes closet at your church or perhaps to a homeless shelter. How about your shoes and purses? Too many?

Oh, perhaps you have clothes that do not reflect Christ when you wear them. What can you do with those items?

Look at your jewelry, makeup, or other "things" you may wear. Ask yourself if this is something that brings honor to God.

We are constantly hit with the message that if you are pretty, sexy, and thin, you wear the latest fashion. Then you are IN! Since the media sends this message out loud and clear, many girls today struggle with wanting to be a certain body type. This can easily become an addiction that leads to very serious problems such as eating disorders. Anorexia and bulimia are deceptive ways of dealing with a poor self-image. Girls start to see their bodies in a different way and harm themselves to achieve "perfection." Before they know it, they are headed down a road of destruction and pain. The mirror and the scales become their God. Satan uses this as a trap. Wake up, girls! Be on your guard. If you notice that you or a friend is starting to go down this road, speak up. Either get help or give help.

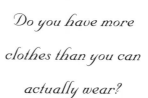

*Do you have more clothes than you can actually wear?*

# GAB Session
## ~ with Chandra ~

A few years ago I was on staff at a church, and I needed a new church outfit for a special Sunday morning. I went shopping and looked until I found the perfect suit. It was black and made out of a stretchy kind of fabric. It had spandex in it but also cotton. (I don't want you to get a picture of me going to church in 1980s aerobic wear.) Anyway, I loved the suit, and it fit very well. It also had leopard fabric around the collar and the cuffs. Well, I got up early, showered, put on my makeup, fixed my hair, and then put on the suit. I was so excited to wear a new outfit, especially one that was so trendy and cute.

Bruce, my husband, hardly ever got up with me on Sundays because I had to be at church for staff prayer at 7:00 A.M. However, this particular morning he got up, admired my new suit, and growled, "You look really sexy today."

Well, I have to admit that comment made me feel really special and beautiful. With the time being 6:30, I knew I needed to hurry so I wouldn't be late.

I started my car and just like every other Sunday morning, I turned up the music and listened to praise and worship music. It seemed to get my mind prepared for the day. This morning, however, was a little different. I couldn't sing along with the music. I couldn't pray. All I could hear in my mind was that my husband thought I looked "sexy."

What would the other men at church think? I prayed," God, if I shouldn't wear this suit, let me be aware of how others look at me today."

When I walked into the room there were about ten men and two women. Within moments, two of the men told me how nice I looked. Then one of the men (who is like a brother to me) said, "New suit, Chandra? Nice!"

"OK, God, I hear you loud and clear." Staff meeting was over, and I walked down the hall to my youth area. I almost felt as though I were naked in church! Needless to say, I never wore that suit again.

**Open your Bible and read Exodus 20:4–6.**
After reading the verses, answer these questions.
Have you allowed clothing to become something you worship? Would you give it up for God? Why or why not?

_____

_____

_____

_____

_____

What drives you or others you know to dress inappropriately?

_____

_____

_____

_____

_____

The Beauty and the Beast in Me

Who should we want to please more—God or our friends? Why?

_____

_____

_____

_____

_____

_____

Why do you try to be someone you're not?

_____

_____

_____

_____

_____

_____

Do you feel a need for acceptance from certain people? Who are these people?

_____

_____

_____

_____

_____

_____

Do you fear rejection? Why?

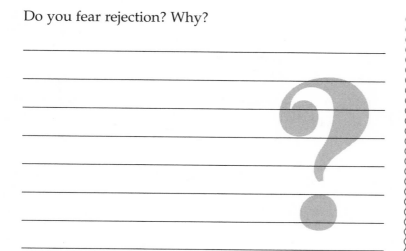

_____

_____

_____

_____

_____

_____

Remember two very important words: **BE YOURSELF!** God created you to be you, not anyone else. Are you trying to be someone else to make everyone like you? Do you fear people won't like the real you, just as God created you to be? How sad it is when we choose to be anyone else but ourselves. How sad it must also make God!

Through our faith in Jesus, we don't need to live in fear. God tells us to cast all our cares upon Him. He will provide for us. God wants us to be the persons He created us to be.

Here are a few more questions to think about.

• What are other reasons you wear a mask and try to be someone else?

• Why do you want to fit in with a group where you can't be yourself?

*Be*

*Yourself!*

- Think about the people you hang out with and how you have to work so hard to fit in with them. Why is it so important to you to be in with that group?
- Now think of the friends you enjoy spending time with. What qualities do they have that make them fun to be with?

Memorize the following verses:

*Confess your sins to each other and pray for each other so that you may be healed. The effective, fervent prayer of a righteous man avails much.*
—James 5:16

*Do not fear, for I am with you; do not be dismayed, for I am your God. I will strengthen you and help you; I will uphold you with my righteous right hand.*
—Isaiah 41:10

*Blessed is the man who perseveres under trial, because when he has stood the test, he will receive the crown of life that God has promised to those who love him.*
—James 1:12

OK, we have read over and over in this study that we are unique. Maybe we will begin to believe just how special we are. Maybe we will learn to be happy and secure in our own skin. There is no one else with our fingerprints, but chances are there are some folks that look similar to us. Look at our families! Take a look. Have you inherited any of your families' features? If so, what do you like about those features? What do you dislike?

Make a list here of the things you have inherited that you like and dislike.

| Likes | Dislikes |
| --- | --- |
|  |  |
|  |  |
|  |  |
|  |  |
|  |  |
|  |  |
|  |  |
|  |  |
|  |  |
|  |  |
|  |  |
|  |  |

Have you ever thought of yourself as a wonderful work of art; as God's masterpiece? Each of us is a one-of-a-kind piece of priceless art handcrafted by the Master Artist.

It is important for us to see ourselves as masterpieces formed, shaped, and loved by God. If we continue to focus on our negatives, the beast within us will steal our joy.

❖

## Something Fun to Do

With some friends, watch *Shrek* or *Beauty and the Beast* and apply it to what we have talked about in this session. It is proven, how we feel about ourselves is the way others perceive us. It comes across in our conversations and the way we carry ourselves. Also the way we talk about others speaks highly of how we feel about ourselves.

Are we confident because of whom we are in Christ? Or, does our confidence come from our looks and possessions? When we have a really good hair day, do we walk with confidence; but when we have a really bad hair day, do we walk with no confidence at all? When we are confident in Christ alone, we're confident no matter what our circumstances.

**Open your Bible and read Jeremiah 17:7 and Jeremiah 29:11.**

Memorize these verses before reading further.

# GAB Session
## ~ with Chandra ~

I heard it all my life. I learned about it in Sunday School, but one day I finally got it. God really does love me. I can really know Him, talk with Him, and have an intimate relationship with Him! How awesome is that?

Look at it this way. Who wouldn't want to be the President's daughter or actress Julia Roberts's sister? Because of who they are and the life they lead, we have all wanted to know "someone" like that. So imagine the day you realize the President and Julia Roberts are no comparison to knowing who you already know—God.

For those of you who, like me, went to church every time the doors were open, you may understand. You hear God loves you all the time, and it ends up just being words. Kind of like blah, blah, blah, blah, blah, blah.

But one day it clicked! It was like an atomic bomb going off in our hearts. Our relationship with God, the Father, the Creator of the universe, isn't just an acquaintance. We really have a personal relationship with Him!

Through our relationship, and through hanging out with others who have discovered His Truth, we have joy. Real joy! Nothing we could buy, or no one we could know, winning the lottery, or nothing, absolutely nothing, can compare with Him. The treasure is already ours.

After figuring this out, I realize there has been a

change in my life. I am content with all that I have. My greatest desire is to glorify Him in all that I say and do. After all, this is my purpose in life.

So, when He called me to start GAB Ministry, I didn't worry what others would say or question whether I am good enough. I find my confidence in Him and totally trust in the Lord with all my heart, and I don't lean on my understanding. *"In all my ways, I acknowledge Him and know that He will keep my path straight"* (Proverbs 3:5–6).

May these words be a testimony of His awesome power and grace to you.

Read Ruth 3:11 (NIV). How does Ruth describe her daughter-in-law Naomi?

A woman of _____

Read Proverbs 31:10–31 to discover what noble character is. What characteristics stand out to you? Writer those below.

_____

_____

_____

_____

_____

_____

# My Journal

Journal your thoughts about someone you consider to be virtuous. This person may be a role model like a family friend, your grandmother, or mother. Now, journal your thoughts about your being a virtuous young woman.

# My Journal

# My Journal

# My Journal

# My Journal

# The Condition of Your Heart

*Everyone has a heart, but the condition of each heart is very different.*

"My heart is broken." Those are the sad words I heard as the teary-eyed girl cried on my shoulder. Regretfully, I have heard these words often from teenage girls who have just broken up with their boyfriends. I have also heard these words from my own mother who lost her sweetheart to cancer after 46 years of marriage. Many times I have heard these words, and can say without question, there is immense pain that accompanies the broken heart.

"He just has such a hard heart. He will never change." These words came from a wife speaking of an alcoholic husband who had repeatedly abused both her and her teenage daughter with harsh words.

"My heart is so filled with love I think I am going to burst," exclaimed a bride after her wedding day.

"She has such a fragile heart," expresses a mother concerned about her hurt daughter.

"He is a man after God's own heart" (spoken of David in 1 Samuel 13:14).

Throughout life we too may experience a joyful heart, a glad heart, a sad heart, a broken heart, a bitter heart, an unforgiving heart, a servant's heart, a loving heart, or even a tender heart.

Write about the condition of your heart today and why you believe that condition exists.

_____

_____

_____

_____

_____

## Now Let's Check Your Heart Rate.

Check your heart now by checking off the words that best describe you most of the time. If you see that you're not very happy, you may want to talk to your parents or someone that you know to be a Christian. See your school counselor if you don't have anyone else to confide in.

- ❏ Depressed
- ❏ Happy
- ❏ Unloved
- ❏ Loved
- ❏ Accepted
- ❏ Scared
- ❏ Secure
- ❏ Feeling like you don't matter
- ❏ Unaccepted

This list could go on and on when we are speaking about the conditions of the heart. We may need to let God do some spiritual surgery in our hearts. Some of us need His tender hand of mercy to heal the hurt, or perhaps in more serious cases, the Great Physician may just need to perform a heart transplant.

The truth is when we are walking with the Lord every day, we give Him permission to change our hearts any time He wants to. What comes from our actions, our mouths, and our feelings is a direct effect of what is going on in our hearts. To have a heart like His we must:

❑ Humble ourselves before Him.
❑ Pray daily that He will renew a right spirit within us.
❑ Let His Word be a light unto our path and a lamp into our feet.
❑ Open our hearts to Him.

Our hearts must be right with God if we want to be more like Jesus. This means confessing our sin, repenting (turning from sin), and putting Jesus Christ first in our lives.

Think of it like this: When we open our hearts to God, we allow Him to take out whatever needs to be taken out and put in what He wants to. When we give our hearts to Jesus, we will have peace no matter what our circumstances may be.

*Through Him we are promised peace that passes all understanding.*
*Good character develops from a direct outpouring of our hearts.*

*The truth is when we are walking with the Lord every day, we give Him permission to change our hearts any time He wants to.*

Character is a quality or trait that distinguishes an individual or group. Think about what character your friends portray. Write down their characteristics, and then think about how you feel about this. Some examples might be that your group of friends is good at including others in the group. Or, maybe your group of friends can be trusted. Perhaps your group of friends sets a good example to others because that reputation is also respected among your peers.

My friends _____

_____

_____

_____

_____

_____

*Character is a quality or trait that distinguishes an individual or group.*

Have you ever been disappointed by someone you highly respected? Someone you thought could do no wrong? When you see or hear something about this person that is not keeping within their character, do you feel disappointed and deceived? Why? Describe those feelings below.

Let's look more closely at the character of Christ, and how we can be more like Him.

Three character traits of Christ worthy of imitating are:

❑ Humility
❑ Compassion
❑ Integrity

In your own words write the definition of these three words.

_____

_____

_____

_____

_____

_____

_____

God puts people around you to help you grow in your faith. Who are these special people that God has placed in your life?

_____

_____

_____

_____

_____

_____

What character traits do you admire in others?

_____

_____

_____

_____

_____

List godly traits that you see in yourself then list those you long to have.

_____

_____

_____

_____

_____

**Open your Bible and read Colossians 3:10.**
What was your "old self" like?

_____

_____

_____

_____

_____

_____

Have you seen changes in your life since you have put on the "new self" in Christ? What are those changes?

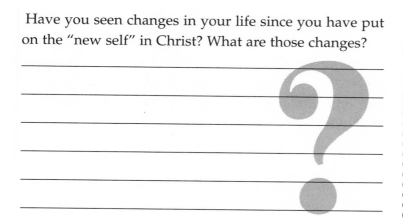

_____

_____

_____

_____

_____

Colossians 3:10 means that in our "new self," we can experience change. We are more like the image of God through Jesus Christ. Just like a baby we must grow, and growing takes time. God loves us so much that He is patient. As we get to know Him better, we will desire to be more like Him. The old thoughts, feelings, words, and actions that came so easily in our "old self," will not interest us anymore.

Let's read 2 Peter 3:9. God is being patient with you. He does not want anyone to be lost, but He wants all people to change their hearts and lives.

Now let's read Psalm 51. This chapter of Psalms shows David crying out to God to help him. David had an affair with Bathsheba that resulted in pregnancy, and to cover it up, he murdered her husband. We're talking major trouble here. Because David's every thought was trying to get out of the sin he had committed, David couldn't sleep, eat, or come face-to-face with God. The sin had become a wedge between him and his relationship with God.

*We are more like the image of God through Jesus Christ.*

Satan loved this! He loved the fact that David was giving in to the stronghold of guilt, being eaten up inside. Finally, David couldn't take it anymore. He knew he couldn't get out of the mess he created so he ran to God and cried out with a heart of repentance. He asked God to take this sin from him, to forgive him.

Now let's look at what God did for David. He showed mercy on him and forgave him. The sin was erased, forgotten. David was washed white as snow. God was right there the whole time David was sinning and trying to cover it up. One sin led to another, but God patiently waited for David to call out to Him. David needed God to rescue him from the dark place he fell into.

Here's the deal. If God forgave David, then God will forgive us too. We tend to categorize sin by putting it in order from worst to OK. Now that's a weird thought, but it is so true. No sin is worse than another in God's eyes.

Now did David still have consequences for his sin? Yes, he did.

Read more of David's story and you will see certain sins may bring about certain consequences, but there is something worse than any consequence we may suffer. Sin hurts God.

**Open your Bible and read 1 Samuel 13:14.**
How did David get the reputation of being a man after God's own heart?
- He was real with God.
- He was willing to obey.
- He served God and not himself.

*Sin hurts God.*

- He was always concerned with following God's will.
- He had a responsive heart.
- His heart was God-centered.

We may think, well, David slept with a married woman, murdered her husband, and sinned against God. And we would be exactly right. But David always ran back to God. He talked to God about everything through prayer. He wanted to do what was right, but somehow continued to fall into sin. Sound familiar?

The fact is, David struggled with many of the same issues we do today. How many times have we said, "I am not going to _____ again"? See, we too do what we don't want to do. We must admit that our flesh is weak.

One word that jumps out at me when talking to just us girls is *gossip*. We girls do have a problem with gossip. But do we get up in the morning and say, "I hope I can hear some juicy gossip today so I can spread it around"?

No, of course not. In fact, just the opposite, we may have gotten up and prayed to God that we wouldn't hear any gossip today, and that we wouldn't start any gossip today.

Let's look at the Bible to see what God says to us about gossip.

Proverbs 11:13—"A gossip betrays a confidence."
Proverbs 16:28—"A gossip separates close friends."
Proverbs 26:20—"Without a gossip a quarrel dies down."

**Also read 2 Corinthians 12:20.**

We girls struggle with this gossip thing. We don't do it on purpose. If we knew the trouble it was going to create, the sleepless nights we would have, and the wrestling in our spirit it would bring, we would never have repeated what we heard in the first place. That is why we need to pray that God will nudge us when we are about to say something we shouldn't. We will hear Him if we are listening. And when in doubt, we can keep our mouths shut! Better safe than sorry.

Why is it that we like to share what we know? We think we can tell one person (just my best friend) and then, we hear the rumor from someone else. Only now, it's twice as bad. That is when we realize that we have started a fire, and it's out of control.

Like David we can make the fire bigger and bigger by adding to it with coals (lies) instead of throwing cold water on it. Admitting that we started the sparks is a very hard thing to do, but it extinguishes the fire before it becomes so out of control that people get hurt.

# GAB Session
## ~ with Chandra ~

Occasionally I have lunch with a group of women from my church. One particular day we got together to celebrate a friend's birthday, but our conversation took a turn. Someone casually brought up a situation that most of us had heard bits and pieces about. Of course I spoke up and shared what I had heard, but to my surprise it was new news to most everyone around the table. So I was heaping coals on the fire instead of throwing water to put it out. I wished at that moment I could have taken the information back because now the new information was spreading fast, and all I heard was "Chandra said, 'Blah, blah, blah, blah, blah.'"

Although I regretted saying what I did, the damage was done. As I drove home feeling sick at my stomach, I knew what I had to do. My heart was telling me that I had to go to everyone that was at that lunch and apologize and ask them to forgive me. My words to them as I made those calls were: "As I drove away from our lunch today, I was convicted for the gossip and deeply regret my actions. Because of this I have added to gossip, which I don't want to be a part of. I need to ask you to accept my apology and ask you to forgive me for my actions. I know I can't take back the things I said so I'd like to ask that you not repeat them. I'd also like to request that from now on when we have lunch that we enjoy our time together and be careful of our conversation."

This was very embarrassing and humiliating, but

The Condition of Your Heart

what a lesson I learned. God was with me as I made each call, and because of my obedience I believe He spoke to others as well. Now I stop, think before I speak, and if I must, I keep my mouth shut.

So be encouraged. I made it through the battle, and God was victorious. He was also glorified because those to whom I confessed could see my heart was humbled and that God had been working in my life. The consequences were hard and the lesson learned was huge. I'm still learning to think before I speak concerning someone else's business. This continues to build the character—which I keep bringing up.

## Write Your Answers to These Questions.

Does the character of your group of friends describe the character you want to portray as an individual? Why?

_____

_____

_____

_____

_____

Do you want people to wonder if you're a Christian or to know you are a Christian? Why?

_____

_____

_____

_____

_____

_____

_____

Do you need to make some changes concerning your character? What would those changes be?

_____

_____

_____

_____

_____

What character changes could you make to bring honor to God:

- ❏ In your group of friends?
- ❏ In your family?
- ❏ In your school?
- ❏ In your youth group at church?
- ❏ In your own heart?

Now let's discuss PRIDE. That is a big word to swallow, huh? Does puffed-up pride fit anywhere in the character of Jesus?

I really didn't think I struggled with pride until recently when I was preparing for a Bible study that brought it to my attention. Guess what? I do struggle with it, and I would have to say that I think we all do at times.

# Take the Pride Test

Do you ever say or think these statements?

- My way or no way.            Yes ❑ or No ❑
- My idea is the best.         Yes ❑ or No ❑
- It can't get done without me. Yes ❑ or No ❑
- Look what I've done          Yes ❑ or No ❑
- I've got the power.          Yes ❑ or No ❑
- I'm in control.             Yes ❑ or No ❑
- I must get the last word.    Yes ❑ or No ❑
- I deserve all the credit.    Yes ❑ or No ❑

All of the above are sure signs of pride. If you checked off even one of the above, you have pride. Jesus never modeled puffed-up pride in His ministry on earth, and He doesn't want us to either.

Look what James 4:10 says, *"Humble yourselves before the Lord, and he will lift you up."*

How do you humble yourself in today's world?
*Humility is a beautiful character of godliness.*

Isn't it a much greater reward to be lifted up in the eyes of the Lord rather than our peers? God has anointed each of us for a purpose. We can depend on Him to give us all we need to complete the task. If He is the One who has called us, given us the task, and equipped us with the tools, then who should receive the glory? God!

Stop and read Acts, chapter 12. In verse 23 King Herod accepted the people's worship, but at the end of the chapter who was victorious?

_____

_____

_____

*Humility is a beautiful character of godliness.*

_____

_____

When God calls us, the Holy Spirit directs His servant (you). The verse in Acts 12 shows that when men become prideful and desire the credit for themselves, God will not allow it. God will not share His authority with another. Herod put himself in a high position and wanted the people to praise him as if he were a god.

Have we ever wanted to be held up, put on a pedestal by our peers because of the leadership role we may have been given? Can we see now how those desires do not come from God? What do we need to remember the next time we have these thoughts?

**Open your Bible and read 1 Peter 5:5.**
Write in your own words what this verse says to you.

_____

_____

_____

_____

There are times when God must show Himself to break the hearts of powerful people. People in leadership who become prideful need to be broken so that God can remind them who really is in charge. Does God still use His power today to bring glory to Himself? Absolutely!

Has there been a time when you have seen the power of God at work? Reflect on that for a moment.

Remember your personal testimony (story) can encourage others to believe. Have you ever had that happen to you?

## Write Your Answers to These Questions.

When you are given leadership positions, what keeps you from being power hungry and controlling?

_____

_____

_____

_____

_____

How do you treat others when you are put into a leadership position?

_____

_____

_____

_____

_____

Do you find it easier to respect the authority of a humble leader rather than a prideful one? Why or why not?

_____

_____

_____

_____

_____

Give an example of both humility and pride in a leader.

_____

_____

_____

_____

_____

_____

We need to pray that God will help us keep a humble heart. We need to be quick to give God the glory for our successes. God wants to pour out His power and blessing on us especially when we continue to give it all back to Him.

Like in James 4:10, *"Humble yourselves before the Lord, and he will lift you up."*

# GAB Session
## ~ with Chandra ~

When Holly, my youngest child, was a toddler she went through a time where she loved to imitate me. When I would yawn, she would yawn. After I would read to her, she would go and read to her baby dolls in Holly language, using the same expressions I had used while reading to her. She would make dinner in her little play kitchen, and I would hear her saying things just like I say them. There she was making comments and facial expressions just like mine.

Getting ready for church one Sunday morning she was sitting on the countertop watching me put on make-up and brushing my hair. Of course she didn't wear makeup at two, but that morning, I put a little powder on her nose and a very light swish with the blush brush on her cheek. She got off the cabinet and ran to Daddy and said, "Look, Daddy. I look like Mommy!"

A few minutes later she came out of my closet with heels on, one of my purses on her arm, and a baby doll over her shoulder. She looked a lot like me only she had a pacifier in her mouth.

Holly loved imitating me, just as I am sure we have imitated others who are important in our lives. What a childlike example of how we (as children of God) should desire to imitate Him.

Matthew 18:1–3 says, *"The disciples came to Jesus and asked, 'Who is the greatest in the kingdom of heaven?' He called a little child and had him stand among them. And he said: 'I tell you the truth, unless you change and become like little children, you will never enter the kingdom of heaven.'"*

*Prayer:*

*Oh, Lord, You have called us to be leaders and we thank You. We ask that Your Holy Spirit will keep us on track and that we will be aware of our selfish pride. Our desire is to be like Jesus—to have a humble heart, a servant's attitude—desiring to give You all the glory and praise. Lord, forgive us when we are prideful and conceited, when we boast of our accomplishments. We ask that You will fill us with the Living Water so that You will shine before men through us. We pray You will create in us a pure heart, oh, Lord. We ask this in the wonderful name of Jesus. Amen.*

## Journal

Journal your thoughts about something you would love to do to make a difference that would be a testimony of Christlike character. Write it below or in your personal journal.

Now, give it to God and ask for His blessing on it. God knows your heart, so if you will take the first step, He will do immeasurably more than you ever dreamed. Go for it!

## Do You Feel the Call?

At the young age of 16 I knew the Lord was calling me to serve Him full time as my vocation. Let me explain. All Christians serve the Lord out of love and obedience to the Father. We serve because it is our joy to do so. Being called to full-time ministry is a little different.

When God called me, it was in a worship service at a youth camp. There were a thousand teens in that auditorium, but it felt as if I were the only one. The Holy Spirit in me was speaking, and I was listening. Not long after that, God gave me a vision where I was speaking to an auditorium filled with students. Since I was 19 years old, I have been working with students in service to the Lord. What a blessing it has been to serve Him! Serving God as I minister His truth to teens is my passion. It's simply who I am.

God seems to be calling more and more girls to surrender to full-time ministry. Hearing the Lord's call on your life at a young age is very exciting! I remember having a lot of questions, yet no one seemed to have the answers. I thought my pastor or Sunday School teacher or parents could get me started, maybe give me some steps on how to begin this journey. Unfortunately I never got clear directions from anyone. Well, at least I didn't think so at the time.

Funny, all these years later I will offer you some of those same words, the godly advice I got from others.

- Stay in the Word and hide those words in your heart.
- Take it step-by-step.
- Keep your focus on Him not them.
- Don't tell God what you want to do, wait for Him to give you passion and clear direction.

I remember walking away from some of those conversations wanting so much more. I wanted a plan. Like a student who goes to college to be a teacher, a doctor, or a pilot, they would receive instructions to be successful at their careers. Do A, B, C, and D, and then you'll be ready. Nope. I finally got it.

His instruction book is the Bible—the holy, living, true, inspired Word of God—and is available to me. I began to study, and He began to teach me. Proverbs 4:20–23 says: *"Pay attention to what I say. Listen carefully to my words. Don't lose sight of them. Let them penetrate deep into your heart, for they bring life to those who find them, and healing to their whole body. Guard your heart above all else, for it determines the course of your life"* (NLT).

God's plan is a learn-as-you-go plan. The more I read, the more I learn. Like chocolate, I crave the Word of God. It fills me up like nothing else. It satisfies my every need.

## Radiant?

As a noted theologian has said, "There are no cookie-cutter ministries."

God used a Christian brother to remind me that each one is called to do something a little different. We are the body of Christ, some the hands, some the feet, and so forth. So we should not try to be like or have a ministry that reflects "another person." Instead we need to desire a relationship so close with Him that He is who we reflect. We need to trust God, stay in the Word, and pray! Pray for wisdom and direction. Pray also for discernment so when people give us advice and direction we'll know when it's from the Lord and when it's not. That's how we can be radiant for Him.

We don't have to be in a hurry. His time is always the best time. He may be calling us today so that He can prepare us for tomorrow, a year from now, or years from now. The key is living our lives for Him today. With a willing heart and a surrendered spirit, when He says, "Move," we will be ready to move.

Read Psalm 37:3–7. We don't have to try and please people or wait for the applause of others. If we do, we'll always feel let down. Instead speak, sing, serve, play sports, teach Bible study, volunteer, or play an instrument for an audience of one—The One. Remember our purpose is to glorify and bring honor to Him alone. How comforting to trust He is faithful to complete His plan.

We should not let others discourage us. Keep the full armor of God on daily. (Read Ephesians 6:10–18.) Find confidence in Him alone. If we do this, we will be ministering out of a pure heart. Our pride won't get in the way. When we make a mistake (which we will), He'll pick us up, dust us off, and send us out again. Praise God for His wonderful amazing grace!

Read Ephesians 3:20. What does this verse mean?

_____

_____

_____

_____

_____

_____

_____

_____

As Christians we are all called to live our lives as a reflection of God. I believe many believers come to a personal relationship with Jesus because they have seen it modeled in the life of someone else. When we model the life of Jesus, we become radiant. When we study God's Word and saturate our lives in it, we become radiant. When we live for Christ and are ready to answer His call when He opens the door, we become radiant.

*May you always be filled with the fruit of your salvation—the righteous character produced in your life by Jesus Christ—for this will bring much glory and praise to God.*
—Philippians 1:11 (NLT)

*When we model the life of Jesus, we become radiant.*

The good things that Jesus produces in our lives will bring His love into us. It's how we become radiant. Others will describe us as radiant when we reflect God's love, forgiveness, peace, mercy, and hope.

Now look in the mirror again. Are you radiant? Hey, it's so you!

# My Journal

Use the journal pages as you begin to see yourself as radiant for Christ. Reflect each day on being radiant for Him.

# My Journal

# My Journal

# My Journal

# My Journal

# My Journal

# A Few Last Words . . .

**D**iscovering that you shine from the inside out when you keep your focus on the Son has prayerfully changed your way of thinking. You are beautiful! You are radiant! Say it out loud: "I am beautiful. I am radiant!"

After reading the pages of this study, I pray you are convinced that looking good on the inside is what makes you shine on the outside. I also hope that you have come to the conclusion that what you wear or how good you look on your best day is not what defines you. No. It's who you are on the inside—who and what you reflect on the outside—that defines you. You should have a better understanding now of how your heavenly Father sees you and no longer have the desire to look like your best friends or the model on the cover of a magazine.

When you consider the demands of a runway model, be happy you don't have to live up to those unrealistic standards. Talk about a self-esteem crusher! Wow! And who sets today's standard of "beautiful" anyway? Plenty of beautiful girls have the same doubts, fears, and insecurities as every other girl. As daughters of the King, we don't have to be fearful or insecure! God, the Creator of all things, calls us Beautiful. Please, take a deep breath and exclaim, "Thank You, Jesus, for making me beautiful!"

Makeup should enhance, not camouflage. Most people who look at you notice your eyes and your smile. Once again, both of these express what is found in the depths of your heart. Do your eyes sparkle and shine with joy? Does your smile show God's love to everyone? If so, they see Jesus in you, and then your life is truly radiant!

Reflecting back over the study, two verses in the Bible stand out. Each describe a very different kind of woman. Which one describes you?

Proverbs 11:22 says:
*Like a gold ring in a pig's snout is a beautiful woman who shows no discretion.*

1 Peter 3:2–4 says:
*When they see the purity and reverence of your lives. Your beauty should not come from outward adornment, such as braided hair and the wearing of gold jewelry and fine clothes. Instead, it should be that of your inner self, the unfading beauty of a gentle and quiet spirit, which is of great worth in God's sight.*

Godly lives speak to people better than words. People are won over by watching pure, godly behavior.

Hopefully the journal pages of this study influenced you to stop and consider your uniqueness and your purpose. And who knows, perhaps there were some areas in your life where you recognized you had no discretion. Oops! It's OK. We all learn by our mistakes. Don't be too hard on yourself. Simply get back on track staying in the Word, spending time in prayer, and keep on keeping on. Looking forward keeps us from dwelling on the mistakes we have made in our past. God has a great plan for your future. Look forward to it with great encouragement.

The term *inside-out* is used many times throughout the study. I'd like to give you one more tool to help you stay in check with this term. Try to get a visual of your heart as you think of the most beautiful garden you have ever seen. Before a garden can produce beautiful flowers or fruit (depending the kind of garden, of course), there has to be some preparations.

1. First, remove all the junk from the soil. Rocks, clay, and trash may be there; and the weeds have to be pulled.
2. Second, till the soil. During this process, the soil is turned over and over so that it becomes soft and the seeds can take root.
3. Third, plant the seeds.
4. Fourth, fertilize the garden. This gives plants and flowers the best chance of blooming to their full potential.
5. Fifth, water the garden. Without water the garden will surely wither up and die.

Whew! As you can see, gardens take a lot of work. They don't become beautiful and sculpted to perfection without the touch of a master gardener. Gardens that radiate brilliant color and landscape have to be groomed and cared for by someone who is passionate about his work. The gardener takes much care and pride in what he plants and grows in the garden. This requires the gardener to be very attentive. He has to stay alert, being sure bugs and other animals don't creep into the garden and destroy the plants.

Now take a better look at the garden within you. Look at your heart. Take a moment and read John 15:1–5. Reflect on what these verses say to you. Memorize these verses.

In verse 1, Jesus says, *"I am the true vine and my Father is the gardener"* (NLT). As Christians we need to spend time with the Master Gardener so that we too can continually grow in our purposes for life on earth.

In verse 5, Jesus says: *"Yes, I am the vine, you are the branches. Those who remain in me, and I in them will produce much fruit"* (NLT). As Christians we should have desire and passion to produce good fruit. What is this good fruit? The spiritual fruit tree is planted in the hearts of those who invite the Master Gardener (Jesus) to come in. When we spend time with Him, He cares for our garden. This fruit is what our life radiates to others. Galatians 5:22–23 reminds us; *"But the fruit of the Spirit is love, joy, peace, longsuffering, kindness, goodness, faithfulness, gentleness, self-control. Against such there is no law."*

The more time we spend with the Master Gardener, the more spiritual fruit we produce. What fruit do you see yourself producing? How can you produce all these fruits of the spirit? How has the Master Gardener tended to your garden lately?

## Sinful Nature

Read Galatians 5:19–20 out loud. What areas of your life seem to get ignored? Think about it. It's sort of like your messy closet or under your bed? Are there places in your life where you keep shoving stuff in or under until one day it explodes and everything is exposed? In other words, nothing is truly hidden. Are there things you are still trying to hide from God? Why?

Don't hide from God. Instead meet with the Master Gardener, and let Him decide where you need to be touched on that particular day or at that particular moment of life. God is there as a loving heavenly father to love and care for you. God is there to help you at all times, no matter what. And His love is unconditional. There will be days when you need tilling. Some days you will need the weeds pulled. And, many days when you need a drink of water because you feel spiritually dry. Then there will be the days when you need some root booster, a recharge to get you going strong again so you bloom and radiate to all those around. Only God can give you the right root booster or recharge—the help, the love, and the drink of water—that you need to help you shine and be radiant for Him.

The beauty of a flower reaching upward in full bloom can't go unnoticed. Are you in full bloom? Why or why not?

Read Philippians 1:9–11. In these verses Paul reminds us of the fruit of our salvation. And may you always be filled with the fruit of your salvation—those good things that are produced in your life by Jesus Christ—for this will bring much glory and praise to God.

Let me remind you once again that God is not impressed with your external beauty; He instead focuses on your inward qualities. How fun to watch a tiny seed grow until one day, to your amazement, it really is in full bloom.

Bloom, little sister, bloom! Be radiant for the entire world to see.

*Chandra*

# More GAB Sessions
## ~ with Chandra ~

### Dear Gabby,

I am 21 and currently living with my boyfriend. I live in Austin and go to the University of Texas. While home for spring break, I saw your column and thought, *finally, here is someone I can ask without feeling judged.* Well, here goes. I haven't gone to church in two years because my boyfriend thinks it's dumb. I guess I have been questioning religion the past two years while at school. But for some reason I feel like nothing is making me happy. Nothing is enough for me. I have been thinking about church on Sundays lately, but I know if I go, he will get mad or something. So what do you think about nothing making me happy, and do you know of any good churches in Austin?

Brandi
Austin, Texas

### Dear Brandi,

I am so glad you asked! First of all, I feel that the Lord is sitting right in front of you, behind you, and beside you. It appears to me that you are being pursued; you just haven't recognized that it's Jesus who is pursuing you. How exciting! Spring break, much like the season of spring, reminds us that all things are new again. Trees, plants, grass—have all been lying dormant for winter. I think I see something sprouting in you—perhaps new growth, or maybe a sprout reaching upwards as if to cry, "Help!" As I look out my window while I write this, I notice some plants are already budding, others are just beginning to have tiny greens peeking out of the ground around the root, and still others are looking pretty gray and dormant. Brandi, just like the sun causes these plants to grow and stretch up toward the sun, God is calling you to reach for the Son, Jesus. He loves you! Yes, there is more to life than always feeling empty! Yes, there is joy in true love. Real love is not controlling. Real love doesn't make fun. Real love doesn't make you feel empty. No. Real love comes from God, and He is the only thing that can satisfy you. It's so cool because it's as though He has allowed you to get to the point where you are desperate for Him. It's like you're hungry; you're thirsty; but you just don't know what for. You are craving His love! Jesus told the woman at the well, *"Everyone who drinks this water will be thirsty again, but whoever drinks the water I give him will never thirst. Indeed, the water I give him will become in him a spring of water welling up to eternal life"* (John 4:13–14 NIV).

So here is what you have to do. First, you shouldn't be living with your boyfriend. There is no condemnation in Jesus. He came to seek and save the lost. Second, don't let moving out put fear in you because fear comes from Satan. God has a plan for your life. He will provide all that you need, especially when you are seeking Him first! So, pack up and move out. He will guide you. His Word will be a light unto your feet. Trust Him, Brandi. Third,

More GAB Sessions

there are many wonderful churches in Austin. Find one that is biblically based and start attending each week.

My prayer is that God will meet your need instantly; that just like in Acts 3, when He healed the crippled beggar instantly, He will heal your hurts instantly with His peace that passes all understanding. The crippled beggar wanted money, but God gave him what he really needed. I believe He will do that for you too. God is so good! I pray that you continue to seek Him.

Joy! Grace! Peace!

*Gabby*

(Chandra Peele)

For additional Scripture reading on this subject, read John, chapter 15, "The Vine and the Branches"; and John, chapter 4, "Jesus Talks to the Woman at the Well."

## Dear Gabby,

I'm a twenty one year old college student and have been dating a guy I'm with for almost two years. I think I'm in love. Recently we have wanted to get more physical than in the past. The reason we haven't is because we both have Christian values. But to be honest, I'm beginning to rationalize "why not" in my mind. I hope I get your reply before it's too late. Help!

## Dear I Think I'm in Love,

OK. From your question I don't think I need to tell you that God designed sex for marriage. I'm pretty sure you understand that. However, you are experiencing a battle with your flesh (human desires). This is a spiritual battle. In the heated passionate moments with your boyfriend let's face it . . . you desire him physically.

Let me start out by sharing a familiar passage of scripture commonly used at weddings.

> *Love is patient and kind, Love is not jealous or boastful or proud or rude. Love does not demand its own way. Love is not irritable, and it keeps no record of when it has been wronged. It is never glad about injustice but rejoices whenever the truth wins out. Love never gives up, never loses faith, is always hopeful and endures through every circumstance. Love never fails.*
> —1 Corinthians 13:4–7

First of all . . . you said you *think* you are in love with this young man. There is a big difference between lust and love. Let's review.

| Love is: | Lust is: |
|---|---|
| Love is forever | Lust is for now |
| Love is tender | Lust is tense |
| Love is priceless | Lust is cheap |
| Love is kind | Lust is selfish |
| Love is patient | Lust is impatient |

Since you *think* you're in love, but you admit having a desire for physical touch you are probably in **lust**. It's normal! Don't beat yourself up. However, be aware of the lures of temptation.

> *Temptation comes from the lure of our own evil desires, these desires lead to evil actions an evil actions lead to death. So don't be misled, my dear brothers and sisters.*
> —James 1:14

(When you have a minute read James 1:12–18.) Don't get too caught up in the word *evil* . . . just call it what it is . . . SIN! Know that lust leaves you empty but "real love" never dies.

> *So, dear brothers and sisters, you have no obligation whatsoever to do what your sinful nature urges you to do, for if you keep on following it, you will perish. But if through the power of the Holy Spirit you turn from it, and its evil deeds, you will live. For all who are led by the Spirit of God, are children of God.*
> —Romans 8:12–14

In other words, God always gives His children a way out. Listen to the Holy Spirit in you. The Holy Spirit is your protector, your guide.

Remember when in doubt, *don't*! Turn away from your temptations. In other words RUN!

A perfect story or visual is found in Genesis 39: 6*b*–23.

In this story Joseph was a teenager who had been greatly favored by the Lord. Potiphar's wife wanted to sleep with Joseph and continued to seduce him with her words. (Joseph was a built and handsome young man.) Now, being a teenager and a guy, you know Joseph was tempted just as any teenage boy today. But he resisted temptation. He wanted to honor his master so he ran from the woman.

Even though Joseph was innocent, he was put into prison. However because he did what was right, the Lord was with him making everything run smoothly and successfully.

Now, you have to read Joseph's story for yourself. It's really good.

The choice is yours. I pray you do what is right in the eyes of your Father and run from sexual sin. What you need to do now is talk to your boyfriend about all this. If he loves the Lord, I hope he will agree to do things according to God's plan for marriage.

What's love got to do with it?
Everything! God is love!

My prayer is that each of you will experience God's love every day.

*Gabby*
(Chandra Peele)

## Dear Gabby,

My dad is a pastor and the church we've been at for six years has terminated him. It's a long story, but I've been struggling with it sense April. I've been playing tug-a-war with God for control over it. I want to control everything, but I can't anymore, I have to give it to God, but every time I do, it seems like I find a way to grab it back. I just got home from a mission trip and God broke me, and he told me to let him handle it, just let go of the control. I'm thinking the biggest struggle may be that I don't want to leave my church. We still live here, and the church is my family. I'm scared to death as to what's gonna happen next. But I have faith in God to help me through it. Help!

Amy—15

North Carolina

❖

## Dear Amy,

What you are experiencing is very difficult. Did you know that when you belong to the Lord, nothing touches you that has not passed through the hands of our heavenly Father. This means that whatever occurs, God has surveyed and approved. We may not know why, nor the value of the painful experience but we do know that it must be necessary as He prepares us to serve others more effectively. In my own life I can clearly see that in each painful experience, there has been a process required that would empty me of my own strength so I could always know His is more sufficient.

You have gotten to that place where you are ready to let it go. You know you can't control it or fix it. You simply must "let go and let God."

After dealing with church hurt for 5 years, my Pastor Robert Emmet said to me, "Five years? You better watch out or you're going to end up like Moses and the Israelites. They only have 35 years on you now. Stop being consumed by what you think people are saying or thinking. Move on. You're wasting life."

Wow! Amazing how someone can say words that pierce your heart right to the core; like a dart thrown at a bulls eyes and hits directly in the center. It's quick. You get it! With God's grace, you can get past this. The choice of when is yours to make. Don't be like me and others who have carried around hurt for years. Choose to but the past behind you. Choose to forgive those who hurt you. Choose to surrender "it" and your life to God.

Amy, do you believe in the promises of God? Then stop trying to figure it out or fix it . . . just let it go. Live in freedom, not bondage to a circumstance.

*"Trust in the Lord!"* (Proverbs 3:5–6)

*"He said to her, 'Daughter your faith has healed you. Go in peace and be free from your suffering'"* (Mark 5:34).

May the words the Lord gave me to encourage you today be like the dart that hit the bull's-eye.

Keep Shinin'!

*Gabby*
(Chandra Peele)

## Dear Gabby,

I have a friend who doesn't believe. He knows there is one God, and he knows all about Jesus, but he still doesn't believe. He says he wants to figure out everything, and then he'll believe it. The thing he has trouble with the most is what happens when someone dies. The whole heaven and hell thing really gets to him. Do you know any Scriptures or have any words to help him believe?
Gina

## Dear Gina,

Faith means believing without seeing. Unfortunately I think we all know people who struggle with faith. It's not something they can see or touch so they choose not to believe it until they can prove it. It can also be frustrating when they know so much about the Bible but won't step out in faith and believe the good news. I have talked to a few non-believers who know more Scripture than I, but they still don't believe. They seem to try their best to disprove the Bible. We should be students and study the Word; however, we should not miss the intimate love letters from God while reading.

Praise Jesus His grace is free! All we have to do is receive the gift of salvation and it's ours. How?

> *For it is by grace you were saved, through faith—and this not from yourselves, it is the gift of God—not by works, so that no one can boast.*
> —Ephesians 2:8

Thankfully we don't have to be a genius intellect that has figured it all out before we can come to Christ Jesus and be saved. Thankfully there is no test to grade. Whew! We should all shout a big "Amen" to that!

Below are some Scriptures you can use when talking with your friend. But first, know that it is not up to you or anyone else to get this young man saved. It is God who will pursue him and offer grace. We simply have to live out our faith as a witness. Shake a little salt and shine the light every chance we get. Second, never stop praying for your friend and others who need Jesus. Third, share Scriptures with him but don't come across as preachy. You could also write verses and give them to him to read, hoping you'll have an opportunity to discuss them later. Here are a few verses to get you started.

### Choose Life!

*This command I am giving to you today is not too difficult for you to understand or perform. It is not up to heaven, so distant that you must ask who will go to heaven and bring it down so we can hear and obey it? It is not beyond the sea, so far away that you must ask. Who will cross the sea to bring it to us so we can hear and obey it? The message is very close at hand; it is on your lips and in your heart so that you can obey it.*

*Now listen! Today I am giving you a choice between prosperity and disaster, between life and death. I have commanded you today to love the Lord your God and to keep his commands, laws and regulations by walking in his ways. If you do this you will live and become a great nation and the Lord your God*

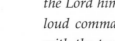

*will bless you and the land you are about to enter and occupy. But if your heart turns away and you refuse to listen, and if you drawn away to serve and worship other gods, then I warn you now that you will certainly be destroyed. Today I have given you the choice between life and death, between blessing and curses. I call on heaven and earth to witness the choice you make, Oh, that you would choose life, that you and your descendants might live! Choose to love the Lord your God and obey him and commit yourself to him, for he is your life. Then you will live long in the land the lord swore to give your ancestors Abraham, Isaac and Jacob.*

—Deuteronomy 30: 11–20

Although this command was given decades ago, I believe it is true still today. We must choose life or death. If we choose Jesus, we choose Life!

Another wonderful Scripture passage to use is 1 Thessalonians 4:13–18:

*Brothers, we do not want you to be ignorant about those who fall asleep, or to grieve like the rest of men, who have no hope. We believe that Jesus died and rose again and so we believe that God will bring with Jesus those who have fallen asleep in him. According to the Lord's own word, we tell you that we who are still alive, who are left till the coming of the Lord, will certainly not precede those who have fallen asleep. For the Lord himself will come down from heaven, with a loud command, with the voice of the archangel and with the trumpet call of God, and the dead in Christ will rise first. After that, we who are still alive and are left will be caught up together with them in the clouds to meet the Lord in the air. And so we will be with the Lord forever. Therefore encourage each other with these words.*

In these 6 verses there is such good news about heaven it makes me want to shout every time I hear it or read it.

**One last tip:** Sharing Christ is about a relationship, not a religion. When discussing salvation, keep Jesus the focus. It doesn't matter what denomination a person is, what matters is the relationship with Jesus.

Does the world see Christ in you? Does your family see Christ in you? What about your school friends and teachers? What about people in your workplace? Today, why not consider yourself a salt shaker.

I Believe!

*Gabby*
(Chandra Peele)

## Dear Gabby,

My mom, who is a Christian, has cancer; and I am really sad about it. What should I do for her during this time? She has chemo treatments and gets really sick. My sister and I don't talk about it too much because we just don't know what to say, how to feel, or what to do. I feel so bad for her and sad for my family, knowing that we might loose her to this disease. Now that the holidays are coming, even though we aren't saying it, we just know it could be our last Thanksgiving and Christmas with Mom. Do you have any help for me?

## Dear Hurting Daughter,

My heart goes out to you. Sometimes hearing testimonies of others who have walked this path seems to bring healing and answers. In the Bible, the book of Acts, chapter 3, Peter and John were going to the temple when they saw a man crippled from birth begging for money. Peter and John didn't have any money, but what they did have they gave to the man. What they had was the power of God in them, which healed the man. In verse 7, the Bible says that, "instantly the man's feet and ankles became strong" (NIV). As you read the rest of the story you see that lives were changed as the crowd witnessed what God had done. Also read John 4:39, and you will see that people believed because of the testimony of the woman at the well. I can't tell you that God will heal your mom, but I can tell you that God has a plan for your mom and for you. The crippled beggar needed more than the pocket change people were putting in his beggar's cup; he needed to walk!

God knows exactly what you need as well. We simply have to put our trust in God. God is still doing miracles. I know this because He does them in my life all the time. Just as Peter explains to the crowd in Acts 3, His power is in those who believe in Him. So, let me share a couple of stories with you. My prayer is that somehow they would be what you need to hear and that you would be encouraged by them.

It doesn't seem that long ago when a very dear friend of mine was "the mom with cancer." She had two very precious teenagers who she knew were somewhat fearful. Every day as she took treatment, she was sick in bed most of the time, had no hair, and all the other yucky stuff that goes along with cancer. Shari was a friend to everyone and touched the lives of many people because of her courage and strength in the Lord. I know that her kids had to go through every emotion there is; however, no matter what they were feeling, they trusted God was holding them just like He was holding their mom.

*The Lord is near. Do not be anxious about anything, but in everything, by prayer and petition, with thanksgiving, present your request to God. And the peace of God, which transcends all understanding, will guard your hearts and your minds in Christ Jesus.*
—Philippians 4: 5–7

Another friend of mine who had just begun her first year of college became ill. After weeks of not feeling well, she went to a doctor who put her in the hospital for more tests. What they found didn't seem good. I stood there with the family while Melissa was wheeled away into surgery, not knowing what the outcome would be. Cancer? Leukemia? Wagner's disease? A virus of some sort? This 19-year-old, beautiful, in-love-with-Jesus young woman was at peace. She listened to the doctors tell her about the "what ifs" with the joy of the Lord on her heart, which shone brightly through her eyes and her sweet smile. She was a blessing to all those who surrounded her as she repeated, in the midst of her pain, "God is good!" Praise God, after a couple of hours, the surgeon announced the problem was not cancer. Just days later, however, Melissa was told she had Wagner's disease. Again, her words to me were: "Chandra, whatever I have to go through, God is with me. God has a plan. God is good!"

So, I guess the best help I have for you is to draw close to the Lord. Let Him hold you in His bosom; take refuge in the shelter of His wings. These times of suffering bring us to a deeper intimacy with God. What would the world be like if we learned to live today as if it were our last? Your mom is here today; so be yourself. Love her, and share your thoughts and feelings with her. The most important thing to your mom, I'm sure, is knowing that if the Lord takes her home, she will see you again someday. The Bible tells us not to worry about tomorrow because today has enough troubles of its own. So give God thanks and live today to its fullest!

Another friend of mine, Carolyn, just days away from meeting Jesus in heaven said these words to me: "Talk about the living not the dying."

And my sweet daddy left these words with me: "Hurry up. Don't wait. Live for God!"

There are many other teens in our community who

have walked down the same road or at least one that looks very similar to yours. For example, there are several ways to get to the Texas panhandle from San Antonio, but each one of those roads must pass through a stretch of dry desert land where you see nothing but a tumbleweed here and there. It seems like a lonely road, but just remember God is with you. Cancer and other chronic diseases are life-changing no matter what the outcome is. I'll be praying for you and your family. Enjoy every moment with your mom. May God bless you and your family with a wonderful and very special holiday season! God's Word is the best gift that I can give you. Read Ephesians 3:20.

## *Gabby*
(Chandra Peele)

# Notes

# Notes

New Hope® Publishers is a division of WMU®,
an international organization that challenges Christian believers
to understand and be radically involved in God's mission.
For more information about WMU, go to www.wmu.com.
More information about New Hope books may be found
at www.newhopepublishers.com. New Hope books
may be purchased at your local bookstore.

# Other Books By This Author

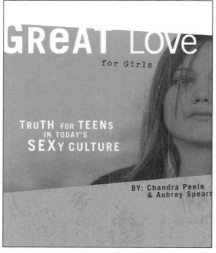

**Great Love (for Girls)**
*Truth for Teens in Today's Sexy Culture*
**Chandra Peele and Aubrey Spears**
ISBN 1-56309-964-0

**Priceless**
*Discovering True Love,
Beauty, and Confidence*
**Chandra Peele**
ISBN 1-56309-909-8

**Great Love (for Guys)**
*Truth for Teens in Today's Sexy Culture*
**Chandra Peele and Aubrey Spears**
ISBN  1-56309-965-9

**Available in bookstores everywhere**

For information about these books
or any New Hope product, visit
www.newhopepublishers.com.